Pamela
Gay-White

BÉJART
AND MODERNISM

CASE STUDIES

IN THE

ARCHETYPE OF DANCE

UNIVERSITY PRESS
OF THE SOUTH

2006

Published in the United States by:

> University Press of the South, Inc.
> 5500 Prytania Street, PMB 421
> New Orleans, LA 70115 USA

E-mail: unprsouth@aol.com   Fax:(504)866-2750   Phone:(504)866-2791
Visit our award-winning web page:
> http://www.unprsouth.com

Visit our partner's web page:
> http://ww.punmonde.com

Acid-free paper.

Pamela Gay-White.
Béjart and Modernism. Case Studies in the Archetype of Dance.
First Edition.

French/Francophone Studies, 14. Theater, 13.
xviii + 178 p.
Includes Bibliography and Index.

1. Dance. 2. Maurice Béjart. 3. Popular Culture. 4. Dance Spectrum. 5. Lausanne. 6. Symbolism.

ISBN: 1-931948-23-2.
Library of Congress Catalog Card Number: 2004106783.

This book is dedicated to the New Orleans International Ballet
Conference, to David,
And to the memory of Kyra Nijinsky

PREFACE

The art of French choreographer Maurice Béjart emerged in Europe in the early sixties in the wake of two developments in theatrical performance: grand spectacle reaching an apogeeé in the opulent stage designs of the *Grand Ballet du Marquis de Cuévas* and in the aftermath of experimentation in form symbolized by dramatists of the absurd who departed from accepted premises of language and stage decor. After reading an earlier draft of this manuscript, an editor complained that he still did not know "why" he should or should not like Béjart. From the sixties to the late seventies, preceding the time frame of his reading, this complaint was typical and shared by many American critics who perceived Béjart's choreographic work as controversial, as going against the grain of established ballet tradition, moreover as narcissistic, abstract subjectivity, and therefore invalid. Yet Béjart's original public, today comprised of older ballet goers, remains loyal.

Following a career which spans the latter decades of the twentieth century, Béjart continues to address his audience through performance which, in its cultural analysis, is an infinite melange of erotic and sacred, of orient and occident, of theatrical spectacle and desiring force. Conceived through the prism of multiple dance vocabularies, Béjart is able to blend diverse stage vocabularies with movement and simultaneously to sustain experiments with language. Béjart's from a point of departure is the dismantling of the literary archetype.

Believing that the emotional response of the crowd, or the popular appeal of a work of art, is as much a factor in its evaluation as the intellectual analysis, I began to research Bejart's contemporary work not as dance, but as spontaneous theater. In an attempt to trace its value in terms of an "alternative tradition" for dance, impacted by late-nineteenth and twentieth century performance macrocosms, I came to the conclusion that what

Béjart proposes for dance is indeed an alternative vision of this art medium.

To better understand Béjart's legacy, two aesthetic techniques must be taken into account which, taken together, cause his works to depart from traditionally conceived notions of ballet: (1) their aesthetic value as choreography favoring long, intricate, solo passages for the male virtuoso; (2) their overly-ornate *mises-en-scène*, containing magical sleights of hand (such as constantly shifting relations of movement to scenic space, coupled with unusual auditory effects, which when juxtaposed, create a total stage form). In awakening our senses, this technique splinters our expectations of dance, dazzling our senses to the point of excess. As one views such works as the full-length *Pli selon pli* or *Notre Faust*, for example, movement is fragmented as isolated phrases, developing finally into a collage of values wielded onto a narrative axis conceived as pictorial frames. This sequence of crafted tableaux created through a stunning display of special lighting and sound effects reminiscent of multi-theater, this dominance of male virtuosity, draws its base from literature and then radically departs from traditionally conceived doctrines of performance.

Maurice Béjart has at times referred to film, rather than dance, as the primary art form of the twentieth century. Thus, in ballets staged in Brussels, Belgium and in Lausanne, Switzerland, he uses techniques of film montage to elicit audience response or suggest a particular point of view. Intertwining cinematic codes suture linguistic and cultural forms in works such as *Dichterliebe* and *Notre Faust*. Through the process of suturing, the spectator or viewing subject may enter into a sequence of performance frames becoming "engaged" in performance process. While remaining cognizant of the "otherness" dictated by the performance space, the spectator nevertheless completes its existence, lending to the act of performance a sense of game and "presentness."

Through his choreography and through numerous essays on mediums of film, theater, and opera, Béjart deconstructs the dance art at its core, then reconstructs it for his purposes. Thus, the *Ballet du XXIème Siècle* and *Béjart Ballet Lausanne* exist as performance facilities which foster not only the study of dance but also the active engagement of dance with sister art forms.

Borrowings from theater and opera, as well as musical scores, predominate Béjart's dance theater, as do mergings of different registers of dance. Béjart's stagings for theatrical companies such as the *Compagnie Rénaud-Barrault* in Paris and for opera houses such as La Scala in Milan bring to their respective performances many diverse elements. This book clarifies the historical premise foregrounding these borrowings through which Béjart's deliberate and compelling destruction of the literary "masterpiece" is revealed as a gesture of modernist representation.

Although Béjart's company, *Rudra*, thrives today in Lausanne, prior to 1984 he was based in Brussels. Béjart, however, is French (born in Marseilles) and his ballets probably inherited their classical dance basis from his own early performances in more traditional companies. With the *Grand Ballet du Marquis de Cuévas* and smaller companies, such as those of Roland Petit and of Mona Inglesby that existed in France and elsewhere prior to the sixties, Béjart learned and practiced a traditional vocabulary of movement.

Theatrically, however, Béjart has ventured further to present unique combinations of elements reshaped from forms dating back as far as symbolism, surrealism, the envisioned theater of Antonin Artaud, and post-war stage experimentation. He has also created contemporary stagings of danced movement in collaboration with such *metteurs-en-scène* as Patrice Chereau and with the Paris-based *Compagnie Rénaud-Barrault*. Through movement rituals conceived, then interspersed within carefully constructed frames, an assertive and spontaneous representation of twentieth century values appears.

Younger choreographers such as Anne-Marie de Keersmaeker, Karol Armitage, and others performing in Europe in the wake of Béjart have followed his daring innovation. Some have chosen to follow in the steps of such American "fathers" as Merce Cunningham and Alwin Nikolais. However, if one analyses Béjart's dance within the aesthetic framework of a European history of multi-theater, his dance project fits into place. By the role he accords movement within the conception of total spectacle, Béjart is a pioneer of dance who parallels the symbolist poets, and innovative dramatists and impresarios such as Sergei de Diaghilev, Edward Gordon Craig, and Antonin Artaud. He both understands and incorporates their legacy into a spectacle form wherein movement, based on ballet technique, is a central stage element toward the creation of a mid-twentieth century *gesamtkunstwerk*.[1]

With an uncanny ability to imitate, yet not duplicate pre-existing styles, Béjart has successfully reworked traditional formulas to fit more modern contexts. In the mid-twentieth century, he showed modern audiences that dance can be as popular as a detective novel and as forceful as a game of soccer. Even his slogans, clichés and fads which, when dramatized, appeared humorous or unnecessary, showed audiences how to understand his work as one man's idealistic imprint on the present.

Béjart's art reveals careful processes of experimentation based on archetypes of religion, social behavior, and history. These not only shape our present, but are exalted through artistic performance of art. One of his former dancers, Diane Grey-Cullert, equates dancing for Béjart with mystical revelation, questioning Béjart's daring restructuring of issues transcending space and time. She questions, "Which world culture or which religion would he next choose as basis for a ballet? Which myths and resultant social contexts would he decipher and thus explore to define new boundaries?"

In defining Béjart's futuristic vision of the mid-twentieth century, a framework emerged that encompassed elaborate experimentation with theatrical elements and that reified intense social and political issues. In each successive work emerges a unique process of experimentation. This plethora of experimental form can claim as one of its most historically direct antecedents the highly individual fusion of scenic elements theatrical works staged by symbolist poets in the late nineteenth century.

Although Béjart today has chosen to abandon large spectacles in favor of small atelier performances, he continues to shift the parameters of dance and embrace other art forms through continued, painstaking research. Whereas in the past he preferred a profusion of spectacular imagery and monumental stagings in his ballet, today he speaks of having realized his ambition. Today

1 *Gesamtkunstwerk* may be defined as a total theatrical macrocosm wherein all arts participate equally as facets of representation, forming a fusion of the art forms of poetry, music, and imitative movement, to which may be added architecture and painting.

Béjart continues to focus his energy on what may be seen as a timeless cycle of beginnings.

While a student at The University of California, Berkeley and simultaneously San Francisco staff correspondent for *Dance Magazine* during the late seventies, I was accorded special permission by Maurice Béjart to tour with *Le Ballet du XXième Siècle* in Paris and in Brussels. During this period interviews with Maurice Béjart, Suzanne Farrell, Dyane Grey-Cullert, Daniel Lommel, Angèle Albrecht, and others were recorded. In examining this time period as Béjart's cycle of beginnings, I believe this study will interest the reader through offering a deeper appreciation of the importance of mid-century modernist essays in dance as well as to cultural studies. Since few of Béjart's large-scale ballets have been performed in the United States, whenever possible, I have differentiated between American and European productions. I have given, whenever possible, careful attention to exact dates and exact locations of theaters.

Finally, each of the five chapters of the present version of this book gives to the reader a singular perspective on Béjart. The first chapter concerns the representation of several of his more important ballets as archetypes of modernism in dance; the second explores his continuation of the tradition of multi-theater spectacle. This chapter also analyzes historical precedents of Béjart's performance by placing them within a system of logical chronological evolution. The third chapter attempts to elucidate formal elements contained in Béjart's repertory. In addition, this chapter presents a chart of possible groupings or categories of works choreographed during a given period, in which characteristics differ. Cumulatively, these three chapters provide both historical background and overview through which Béjart's art may become more clearly accessible.

The final two chapters of this text contain personal impressions of Béjart, impressions derived from interviews with dancers and from my recorded conversations with Béjart in visiting Brussels and Lausanne between 1974 and 1993. Importantly, these chapters contrast Béjart as artist from the point of view of journalists and scholars with the more intimate point of view of his dancers.

This chapter opens with an exploration of mid-seventies works performed in Brussels, including *Serafita/Serafitus*, the full-length version of *Golestan*, and *Pli selon pli*. Since research for this book was gleaned from documentation in French from Belgium and France, I have translated this material into English. I have also translated in English texts for multi-lingual verses of Béjart's ballets, where non-musical vocal sound resonates and is interspersed with musical score.

This section couples interviews with dancers with personal observations made during a series of visits to Belgium in the late seventies. The five dancers who were closest to the choreographer at the time, and for whom many of his more important works were created, generously gave their time. Some are today directors of companies or are major ballet stars. The interviews, together with research of dance history, are intended to make the presence of Béjart more immediate to the reader.

The final chapter, *L'Autre Chant de la danse,* takes as its point of departure Béjart's autobiography. It is a commentary on the choreographer's life encompassing Béjart's imaginings and his dreams. Between the lines of this text is the idea that dance, and particularly that of Béjart, can represent the ideals and aspirations of a given culture through revealing the immediacy of modernity. Perhaps this is Béjart's purpose in creating for the art he has termed the most singular of our century. It is my hope that a careful perusal of pages describing some of Béjart's lesser-known works will interest readers to further experience and explore his achievement.

I would like to express special appreciation to Dr. John Erickson of the University of Kentucky at Lexington, Dr. Pamela Paine of Auburn University, and Dr. Barbara Hayley of Tulane University, New Orleans for their active support of the publication of this book. Special words of thanks are also due to friends and colleagues, Dr. Charles Craig, Dr.Garrett McCutchan, Dr. Fred Lippincott, and Ms.Kathleen Stites of Baton Rouge, who both read the manuscript and offered invaluable suggestions and corrections for the final version. In addition, the encouragement, support, and advice from Mrs. Curt (Elisa) Goodson, formerly of the Department of Romance Languages at Queens College of the City University of New York, has been invaluable. Especially

INTRODUCTION

Maurice Béjart was born in Marseilles, January 1, 1927, the son of industrialist and philosopher of education, Gaston Berger. His father abandoned his own university studies at an early age to serve as a volunteer on several fronts during World War I. Berger's heroic acts earned him numerous medals including the *Croix de la Guerre*, the *Croix du Service volontaire*, and the *Médaille de l'Orient*.. Following his return, Berger became part of a small Marseilles enterprise and, at the same time, studied painting and musical composition. Late in life, he reentered the university and obtained a *Diplôme d'études universitaires générales* in philosophy. Berger's avid curiosity, perseverance, and engaging personality as lecturer and scholar slowly transformed his business career into that of university professor. He authored many texts, among them, *L'Homme moderne et son éducation*, that are today regarded as exemplary within the annals of French education.

Berger's dedication toward self-betterment influenced his son, Maurice, at an early age. He allowed the young Maurice intellectual choice, a freedom not usually accorded classmates of the young boys of the social milieu of Marseilles. Béjart and his sister could leave their house on the rue Ferrari as often as they pleased, could read what they chose, and, more importantly, could sit at dinners given for family friends who were often prominent intellectuals. Remembering frequent eavesdropping on such conversations, Béjart today describes how at "every lunch, my father had students, teachers, great philosophers, friends, and intellectuals who would come to visit from India or from China. Every day, I could sit at the table and pick up bits and pieces of conversations. It was my father's way of life, his daily habits, that I remember."[2]

Today, Béjart remembers three chronological periods during which his father served as an influence. First, when they lived together as father and son at their house in Marseilles on the rue Ferrari; second, when Béjart moved to Paris and began a career as a dancer; and third, when, as an adult choreographer, he studied his father's

---

2 Personal Interview: Maurice Béjart. Brussels, March, 1975.

father's texts as a basis for ballets. Ballets he choreographed before the founding of the Brussels-based *Ballet du XXième Siècle*, such as *Suite viennoise,* featured the texts not only of Berger, but also of Albert Einstein, and of Jesuit visionary Pierre Teilhard de Chardin. These early works reveal the presence of a strong spiritual bond, one linking father to son.

At age eight, Béjart experienced the sudden death of his mother, an event that foreshadowed a childhood retreat to the realm of the theater. Through avid readings of texts of Porto-Riche, Bernstein, and Edmond Rostand, the theater became an aspiration that compensated for the loss of his mother. The young boy dreamed of becoming a director and so, between twelve and eighteen, read profusely works by the writers Jacques Prévert, Charles Baudelaire, and Guillaume Apollinaire. He also wrote collections of short novellas and poetry. Then, because of his frail health, his father enrolled him at age thirteen in ballet classes. In *L'Autre Chant de la danse,* his autobiography of dreams, he writes:

> J'ai quatorze ans et je monte en courant les six étages d'une maison près du port à Marseille. Arrivé au cinquième je m'arrête soudain, non pas tellement pour souffler, bien que mon coeur batte très fort, mais surpris par une sensation nouvelle, joie et panique, plénitude dans l'attente et cependant envie de rebrousser chemin. Une angoisse subite qui est aussi bonheur, et je découvre là sur ce palier, un compagnon qui ne devait plus me quitter ensuite: le trac.[3]

> I am fourteen years old and quickly ascend six flights of stairs of a house near the old port of Marseilles. On the fifth floor, I stop, not just to catch my breath, although my heart is beating heavily, but surprised by a new sensation, panic and joy, ecstasy in the anticipation and desire to turn back. A sudden anguish that is also happiness, and I discover there, on the platform, a companion who will never leave me: stage fright.

---

3 Maurice Béjart. *L'Autre Chant de la danse* (Paris: Flammarion, 1974), 182.

The courage to travel to Paris to pursue a career, to dare to go beyond Marseilles, the mystical domain of the father, and of a childhood shadowed by loss, is embedded in Béjart's psyche. In the same text, he describes his first dancing class:

> Je monte vers ma première léçon de danse au dernier étage d'une de ces grandes maisons du XVIIe siècle dans l'ancien quartier des Galères. Un large escalier en bois, tournant à l'angle droit dans une cage d'escalier carrée, débouchant sur une galerie en grosses poutres de chêne, déjà l'entrepont d'un bateau, et là au sixième étage, derrière une petite porte rouge sombre: le studio de danse. Une salle rectangulaire tapissée d'un papier peint à fleurs orange. Deux fenêtres donnant sur deux rues différentes d'où montent les cris des marchandes de coquillages. Un vieux piano, presque toujours muet car la pianiste ne vient que le jeudi. Un miroir miniscule dans un cadre noir et or et sur trois côtes de la pièce, fixée au mur: la barre. [4]

> I climb to the last floor of one of the large, seventeenth-century homes in the ancient *Galères* quarter for my first dance lesson. A large wooden staircase, turning at right angle to enclose a square-framed stairwell, opening onto a gallery in large oak beams, the mid-deck of a ship; and there, on the sixth floor behind an obscure red door is the dance studio. The studio, a rectangular room decorated with orange-flowered paper, is framed between windows that look out on two different streets from which merchants of shellfish cry their wares. In the studio is an old piano, nearly always silent, since the pianist only came Thursdays, a miniscule mirror with a black and gold frame on three walls of the room, and attached to these walls: the *barre*.

Shortly after commencing ballet studies, Béjart joined the *corps de ballet* of the *Opéra de Marseille*. Soon no production took place without his participation. In 1944, he left Marseilles for Paris where he studied ballet under Leo Staats, then professor at the *Paris Opera Ballet*. In Staats he found a severe yet generous taskmaster who considerably forgot to ask him the fee required for lessons. He was

---

4 Ibid, 183. Hereinafter abbreviated as *LC*.

poor and, to survive financially, accepted whatever work was available, often in nightclubs and cabarets. During this period, he appeared at scores of auditions, including the *Opéra Comique*. Actor/director Jean-Louis Barrault describes one such audition:

> En 1946, pour monter la pantomime complète des "Enfants du Paradise": *Baptiste,* je cherchais un Arlequin. Après quelques auditions, je remarquai deux jeunes gens: Marcel Marçeau et Maurice Béjart – Marçeau fit Arlequin.
> Quelques années plus tard, Béjart me confia que cette aventure manquée avait orienté sa carrière. Quelle chance pour lui et pour nous tous! [5]

> In 1946, in order to produce the complete production of the drama, *Les Enfants du paradis,* I looked for a mime to perform the role of Baptiste. After several auditions, I singled out two young men: Marcel Marceau and Maurice Béjart. I chose Marceau .
> Several years later, Béjart confided that this lost opportunity had oriented his career. Happily so for him and for us all!

This was the first of several career beginnings which Béjart undertook as performer. For the company *Théâtre Cirque de Rouen,* he created his first choreographic work, based on a Chopin *Etude.* He continued to experience the ballet repertory when, in 1947, he toured Portugal with the *Compagnie de Ballet de Solange Schwartz.* The same year, he also toured Germany and France with Janine Charrat, former principal dancer with famed choreographer Roland Petit.

To understand Béjart's first attempts as a dancer is also to better understand his ascent as choreographer. In Paris following the Second World War, work for performers, except for that offered by the lavish *Opéra de Paris,* was practically non-existent. After performing one season with the *Ballets de Roland Petit,* Béjart

5. Jean-Louis Barrault, quoted in *Béjart,* Marie-Françoise Christout.. (Paris: Seghers, 1972), 132.

accompanied Yvette Chauviré, then *danseuse étoile* of the *Opéra* to London to perform in *L'Ecuyère* of Lifar.

In order to learn the demanding technique of this most classical of schools, the British, whose standards were higher than those of the French, Béjart remained in London. There he trained under Vera Volkova, famed instructor of the Royal Danish Ballet. In London, he joined the International Ballet of Mona Inglesby with whom he toured not only Great Britain, but the continent as well. He credits this experience as inspiring him to create one day an internationally based company that would travel.

In September 1949, Béjart went to Stockholm to rehearse for a November tour with Birgit Cullberg's *Royal Swedish Ballet*. There, he created his first vision of *L'Oiseau de feu*, a filmed ballet whose theme of a firebird, resistant to capture, reflecting the truth of freedom, he would successfully repeat as *leitmotif* throughout his career. After a period of compulsory military service, Béjart again found himself in Paris.

He realized his dream to found a company of his own in 1953 with the creation of a small concert company, *Les Ballets Romantiques*, a company that he based in Paris. In 1954, after the company performed at the *Théâtre de l'Etoile* its name became *Les Ballets de l'Etoile*. Commencing with a varied repertoire gleaned from the narratives of such diverse sources as William Shakespeare (*La Mégère apprivoisée*), the Bible (*La Nuit de St. Jean*), and electronic music scores composed by Pierre Henry (*La Symphonie pour un homme seul*), the company played to seasons where a Chopin-based repertory became its most popular box office draw. Béjart performed as solo dancer. Among the roles he danced were the lead male role in *La Symphonie pour un homme seul*, and "Puck" in Mendelsohn's *Le Songe d'une nuit d'hiver*.

Whereas the majority of ballets in the repertory of the *Ballets de L'Etoile* consisted of literary works by William Shakespeare performed to Chopin, Pierre Schaeffer, a young French composer who attended these first performances, became interested in the possibilities of classical ballet performed to electronic music. Schaeffer saw a classical performance of the standard "Chopin-Shakespeare repertory" and suggested that a ballet performed to electronic music scores could be developed by him and his protegé, Pierre Henry as an addition to the repertory. Béjart consented. The result was *La Symphonie pour un homme seul* whose signature became its musical score coupled with a sparse set design consisting solely of dangling ropes from the ceiling of a stage, accentuated by deeply-toned blue lighting. Innovative *décor* complemented angular movement designs conceived by Béjart in a performance that caused the popularity of the tiny company to soar. In 1957, Béjart thus became the first European choreographer to work with electronic music

In the same year, Béjart founded the *Ballet Théâtre de Paris*, a company based in Paris that, in order to survive, toured throughout Western Europe for nine months to be able to perform in Paris for three. In summer months, its Paris audiences consisted mainly of tourists since, during that season, the traditionally conservative Parisian public accustomed to ballet performance rarely attended performances of small companies like Béjart's. The result was a company that based itself in Paris to perform for a public essentially non-Parisian. For five years, the company adapted the plan of touring while making Paris its home. During this period, Béjart met Maurice Huisman, newly appointed director of the *Théâtre Royal de la Monnaie* in Brussels, an encounter that served as a turning point, both in his own career as choreographer and in that of his company. Eventually he would form from this small company of dancers, the much grander *Ballet du XXième Siècle*.

In 1959, Huisman asked Béjart to create a major ballet work for a summer festival in Brussels. For this production, he was to select dancers from three companies based throughout Western Europe: from his own *Ballets de L'Etoile*, from the resident Belgian troupe at the the *Théâtre Royal de la Monnaie*, and from the *Western Theater Ballet* of London. From these three companies, Béjart selected the principal dancers who would perform his own choreographic version of the famed *Le Sacré du printemps*, first choreographed in 1914 by Nijinsky. The Brussels press described the December 9, 1959 première:

> Béjart has realized a first-class ballet...which makes its mark in the annals of history...One must remember that even Stravinsky intended to join the chaos of an earth in ferment to primitive rites and the troubled gaze of a virgin goddess who waits for the sun and the harvest.
> Only dancers stripped of all "civility" and formal movement can translate sensations of joy and rapture springing from this adoration of the earth, which in turn is pitted against warrior joustings of rival tribes. Béjart has pushed forward, in an affirmative ascent, the basic syntax of solidly structured choreography.[6]

Bejart's describes his emotional philosophy of dance as "giving dance to everyone." In essence, he has named dance as the free-seeking aspect of culture, an art of idealization able to draw from coexistent aesthetic currents of the past while forging for the future a synthesis that can give to the century's legacy of expressiveness its due. In the mid- seventies, he was supported in this view by Marxist philosopher and literary critic, Roger Garaudy, who perceived Béjart as legitimate heir to prime-movers of modern dance: Isadora Duncan, Mary Wigman, Doris Humphrey, and Martha Graham. Moreover, Garaudy asserted that dance, such as it was envisioned by Béjart, was the sole art capable of summoning a life force and philosophical alternative to the despair posed by authors of the post-war, avant-garde theater.

Reminiscent of statements made by Antonin Artaud in the manifesto, *Le Théâtre et son double*, that true dance and consequently true theater were yet to be born, Marxist Roger Garaudy referred to Béjart's dance as a "spontaneous happening, an event through which to reshape our lives through spontaneous dance or "play". In his text,

---

6 Quoted from *Le Bruxelles Soir* December 9, 1959, 13. Translation mine.

Le Futur altérnatif, Garaudy suggests that, instead of just "constructing our lives, we envision them as worthy of being danced."[7]

Béjart's *Ballet du XXième Siècle* stems from the same cries of revolt that nurtured youth movements of the sixties. Through its popular appeal and theatrical impact, the company became during this period the first to feature long-haired dancers clad in flesh-colored leotards. During the mid-century, Bejart's company came into being as the first to break rules of costume or codes of traditional ballet performance governed by strict technical syllabi, and finally, to rebel. This cry of revolt; this leveling of commonly-conceived codes of performance; this force accorded the role of signification in dance, in fact, reestablished its tradition. In defiance, dancers first performed in flesh-colored leotards, shocking audiences and giving to ballet performance an effect of majestic semi-nudity. Men wore long hair and they, unlike their ballerina partners, were the featured stars.

In this same period, Béjart created a school, the Mudra Academy of Brussels that trained dancers to view all of the arts as a common unity of performance. In this school, established first in Brussels and later in Dakar, Senegal, special attention was given to exercises in percussive rhythms and voice in order to see the body as resonator of sound, and as a locus from which is also directed a particular movement or *geste.* Onstage, a synthesis of vocal pitch and movement become a dominant value, sustaining mood and enhancing narrative of Béjart's early work.

Curiously, the rebellious character of Béjart's early choreographies gave to his European audiences an absolute choice: when Béjart depicted ballets they did not wish to see, they spoke up, rejecting performances of his company and, in so doing, offered their patronage to more traditional companies. Conversely, Béjart's company attracted during the seventies many second generation dancers -- Monet Robier, daughter of Rosella Hightower of *Les*

---

7 Roger Garaudy. *The Alternative Future.* trans: Leonard Mayhew (New York: Simon & Schuster, 1972), 7.

Grands Ballets du Marquis de Cuévas; Lorca Massine, son of famed *Ballets Russes* choreographer Léonide Massine; Isabelle Babillée, daughter of Jean Babillée, star of the *Ballets de Roland Petit*; and Nikolas Ek, son of choreographer Birgit Cullberg -- all of whom had rebelled against their parents' art and were enamored of the new approach then offered by Béjart. During a rehearsal of *I Trionfi di Petrarca* in Paris in the late seventies, Monet Robier declared, aptly: "I would rather dance in the streets than not dance with Béjart."

Before its first U.S. appearance at the Brooklyn Academy of Music in 1969, Béjart's company had gained a reputation in Europe and abroad as a company of soloists that included, among others, American Balanchine ballerina Suzanne Farrell. Whether their respective talents were used to the greatest potential collectively or individually is open to debate. Nevertheless, these dancers, diversely trained and talented, danced together, and created a company which could travel the world, presenting different approaches to performance.

Farrell once remarked over coffee at the canteen at *Mudra,* that perhaps she had experienced the best of both worlds. There could never be another Georges Balanchine who, more than any other twentieth century choreographer, built and trained a company, creating a unique American style from the tradition of its Russian past. "Béjart," Farrell remarked elliptically, reflecting on the dance of today, "was perhaps a man of its future."[8]

Béjart's genesis as choreographer from 1955, when he became the first classical choreographer to use electronic music as a basis for dance, has always contained conspicuous elements of change. Beginning with his Brussels-based *Ballet du XXième Siècle*, through his contemporary *Béjart Ballet Lausanne*, he has proven that he is an artist able to render change and actively influence contemporary taste and criticism. In Europe, the eclecticism of his performance style has caused the public of more traditional companies to grow. In the

---

8 Personal Interview: Suzanne Farrell. Brussels, December, 1974.

United States, he has dared audiences to consider the possibility of an alternative tradition for contemporary, danced performance.

CHAPTER ONE
A STUDY IN POPULAR CULTURE:
MODERNISM AS *MÉTISSAGE*

I argue that a specific historical formation of the category of the literary
developed under the pressures of modernity in such a way as to locate
meaning --- that which had become fractured in the development of
communicative technologies – in the word alone.[9]

In seminal theatrical works of Belgian choreographer Maurice
Béjart, the modernist concern with the artist as hero predomninates,
as does an attempt to reveal the modernist concern with the locus of
meaning existing beyond the literary and "verbal dialogue" of a
subject. This chapter will argue that the modernist concern with
form and with dialectically arrived-at meaning reveals itself in early
works of the seventies and eighties choreographed by Béjart in such
works as *Notre Faust* and *Dichterliebe*. The themes of these and other
heroic ballets choreographed by Béjart during this period represent
the male as poet and dancer, dominant and possessing the ability to
observe and thus to transcend and conquer, and more important to
communicate dialectically through the emblem of the body.

This chapter discusses how modernist concerns are revealed
by Béjart through what he has termed *métissage*, which I define as an
artistic borrowing of many forms and styles, which are at once
spectacular and dependant upon the autobiographical signature.
Derived from the archetype of the literary text, Béjart interjects
personal elements that have marked him the strongest, creating a
fusion of intense dance and theatrical forms.

Modernistic elements in the stagings of French choreographer
Maurice Béjart return to one essential code which is that of *métissage*

---

9 Julia A Walker. "Bodies, Voices, Words: Modern Drama and the Problem of the
Literary" in *Bodies, Voices, Words*. Eds. Jani Scandura and Michael Thurston (New
York: New York University Press, 2001), 69.

or fusion of many diverse elements, creating onstage an anarchic interdependence of creative forms, of which the strongest and least inhibited element is dance. In his particular use of this hybrid form, he might also be called a borrower, albeit one whose choices are entirely subjective.

When questioned during an interview, "Why haven't American audiences understood you?" Béjart responded that the American public that would be enthusiastic for his ballets had rarely been touched, adding that he had, in the States, attracted a very sophisticated audience accustomed to standard "ballet" performance, that was uninterested in his concerns:

> I was never deceived by America....but most of the time, we have had the wrong public. In the city of Paris which is much smaller than New York, when you see the generous amount of people we have without using the public from the Opera, you are amazed. In New York, no one has touched the great audience.[10]

Béjart's American public was one he still searches to define, amid a history or performance whose American criticisms were fraught with controversy over its legitimacy and origin. As it existed in the mid-twentieth century, evolving from the 1960s until the mid-1980s in Brussels, to one of smaller scope and stature in Lausanne, Béjart's *Ballet du XXième Siècle* and its derivatives can today be said to encompass an arbitrary, yet highly expressionistic mixture of forms. As a macrocosm of multi-theater, Béjart's work is at once derivative and heir to such diverse performance groupings as early twentieth century spectacle balletic works of the *Grand Ballet du Marquis de Cuévas* and, on the theatrical spectrum, minimalist stage designs of the post-war theater. In addition his works are centered around precise forms that echo previous systems of multi-theater:

---

10 Personal Interview: Maurice Béjart. Brussels, 1979.

- Concerns of dramatist and visionary Antonin Artaud presented in separate manifestos that rely on the principle of "cruelty" as an intent to arouse or shock describe the relationship of the stage, and – in following – of *mise-en-scène* to a magical, almost hallucinatory realm.
- In the early 1920s, a *gesamtkunstwerk* wherein all arts contributed to the shaping of a staged event conceived around dance as a central element, was witnessed in first Parisian performances of Diaghilev's *Ballets Russes.*
- Elliptical forms and vocal emanations contained in late-nineteenth century staged plays of Symbolist poet-*metteurs-en-scène* resulted in a fluidity of meaning derived from engagement of all of the senses to create a combined "effect" on the spectator.

Although Béjart would later abandon theatrical ballets of great scope replete with ornate stagings and massive troups of dancers for works of smaller dimension (to be based in Switzerland at Rudra-Béjart-Lausanne, a research-centered atelier), these latter *ballets aux multiples danseurs, cette profusion de moyens pour laquelle j'ai toujours eu la plus grande inclinaison et à quoi j'ai donné toute mon énergie*[11] (ballets with many dancers, this profusion of means toward which I have always been inclined and given all of my energy) with their ability to empower their audience through the interplay of elements conceived by Béjart are worthy of attention as unique examples of dance as a principal element of a staged theatrical event.

At the time of the production of *Notre Faust* and *Dichterliebe,* as works to be discussed in this chapter, Béjart's acclaim in Europe was at an all-time high. As the *Ballet du XXième*

---

11 Excerpt from avant-propos to *Pyramide.* Choreography Maurice Béjart. *Palais du Congrès.* February, 1991.

Siècle disbanded in Brussels during the mid-1980s to re-establish itself in Lausanne, and American choreographer Mark Morris succeeded Béjart in Brussels, classics orginally staged in Brussels were recreated on the Swiss-based company, despite the fact that the newer company lacked the eclectic array of soloists which had stunned audiences in earlier decades.

Nevertheless the American controversy over Béjart's early work performed in the United States and the controversial reviews stemmed from an essentially "anglo-saxon" dichotomy in the words of a British journal : *Maurice Béjart n'a jamais fait l'unanimité dans les pays anglo-saxons.* (Maurice Béjart has never won popular acclaim in English-speaking countries). [12]

Certainly American modern dancer-choreographer Merce Cunningham typified Béjart's early work, defined for Europeans, as essentially balletic, but as also serving the purpose of orienting European postmodern dance, such as that seen in then younger companies such as the ballets of Karol Armitage and those of German choreographer Pina Bausch, toward American models.[13] In The United States, critical controversy of decades of the mid-twentieth century stemmed from the strict identification of ballet as a form derived from a classical base, traced to the syllabi of academic schools brought into full play by the choreography of George Ballanchine or, as in the case of modern dance, a free-seeking aspect of culture which had, itself, evolved through several stages of development to the present. To understand the dichotomy between Béjart's acclaim in Europe and the mid-century controversy accorded his dance in the United States is to cite reviews such as that written in the mid-seventies by Robert Pierce of the ballet, *Golestan*, wherein he describes a "series of ritualized mating dances"[14] and, in the same

12 Anne Cendre, "Maurice Béjart divise la critique londonienne," *24 Heures,* 31/3/93: 49.
13 Personal Interview: Merce Cunningham. San Francisco, 1979.
14 Robert Pierce, "When Cultures Collide," *Soho Weekly News* 31/3/77: 20.

review, lauds the "charged ambiance of a performance so vibrant and a wonderful assault on the senses."

In her essay "Dance," historian Sally Banes traces the evolution of postmodern dance in the latter twentieth century through several distinct phases emanating from modernist concerns. According to Banes, early postmodernists first sought to purge historical modern dance through urgent reconsiderations of the medium. Citing the work of Merce Cunningham (whose vigorous movement, style, and use of chance to cause elements of décor, music, and staging to interweave with the choreography, as pivotal between modernism and postmodernism), Banes describes the work of early postmodern choreographers such as Douglas Dunn, Steve Paxton, Simone Morris, Molissa Fenley, and others, as being one of defining dance through a variety of contemporary themes worked into the fabric of the art form itself.

Distinct chronological periods of American dance emerging in the early seventies dealt with analysis of dance, in which the interior view of the dancer became more important than visual, aesthetic standards. This period was followed by one aiming at movement as a metaphor for the disintegrative technological expansion of consciousness. A final period emerges in which narrative content of a danced work becomes re-emphasized. Banes's acute analysis of postmodernism in American choreography is important precisely because, even to European audiences today, Béjart continues to remain a case apart, weaving through simple classic step variations (such as his preferred signature the *dégagé à la seconde*) austere intellectualism and subjective idealism. Béjart thus joins to his cause few disciples among younger generations of European choreographers and *metteurs-en-scène*. These have chosen to seek their models among American postmodern pioneers described by Banes in her essays: Merce Cunningham, Alwin Nikolais, Lucinda Childs, and others. What Béjart accomplished in Europe in the decades of the sixties and seventies was not a choreographic revolution but a sociological one, that of bringing to dance a new audience and one which declared it as captivating as a detective novel, as evocative as cinema, and with as much force as a rugby match. Within Béjart's *corpus* of ballets, definitions cease, as tradition and experimentation are mixed into a performative *métissage*, although, at times, the effects of this mixture have been "jarring."

In the early seventies Marxist philosopher Roger Garaudy,[15] in his primary text on popular culture, *Danser Sa Vie*, comments upon the unique contribution of Béjart to contemporary performance. Therein, Garaudy describes that "to dance one's life" is indeed to make of the dance form envisioned by Béjart, a prospective art in its attempt to synthesize the past through a creation portending the future:

> La danse prospective de Maurice Béjart, dans son effort constant pour participer à l'invention du futur – pas seulement de l'avenir de la danse mais de l'avenir de l'homme – ne nie pas non plus le passé: elle en intègre au contraire les créations. [16]

> The prospective dance of Maurice Béjart, in a constant effort to participate in the invention of the future--not only of dance, but of man as well--does not deny the past; it enjoins to the contrary, creations.

In choosing the term "prospective," Garaudy linked Béjart to major developments of twentieth-century dance and, in particular, the aesthetic of dance represented by early pioneers: Mary Wigman, Doris Humphrey, and Martha Graham. The role he gives to Béjart in this progression is consistent with the progression of modern dance movement forms.

For modern dance pioneer Doris Humphrey, Garaudy summarized, the first task of the choreographer was to nourish

---

15 In 1968, Marxist philosopher Roger Garaudy made headlines as supporter of the Communist invasion of Czechoslovakia.
16 Garaudy, *Danser Sa Vie*, (Paris: Editions Seuil, 1973), 170-71. My translation.

himself with the energy of the world in which he lived. For Humphrey, this inspiration proceeded from diverse observations of daily life forming itself into a new civilization. The gestures of daily life were thus inspired by giant cities, and dominated by angular lines and roaring machines. Humphrey's fundamental rhythm, expressed in her choreography, was one of constant conflict between man and his physical environment. Humphrey expressed this conflict through a movement dynamic which constantly resisted weight. A symbol of the exterior forces made by man can be seen in such choreographies as *New Dance* (1935) and *Theater Piece* (1936).

For Mary Wigman, dance centered around an even more limited idea of space wherein, through breathing, the dancer could create postures which conquered countless constraints. For Wigman, the use of space was both vital and limited. The exterior forces of environment could cause the body to "react in tension" and thus to subject itself to constraints. Since this environment engendered mystery and a sense of unknowing, dance was based less on continuity and stability of form than on rhythm. It was an effort to seize life's ephemeral, emotional realm.

For Martha Graham, expressiveness shown in choreography was often based on characters from Greek mythology. In Graham's choreography of *Cave of the Heart*, the dancer-actor as Medea seeks to communicate emotions from within her own emotional ranges. In turn, she attempts to project a freedom or space beyond the perimeter of the dance. Formed from both the gesture itself and from its full projection into space, Graham's dance became the physical embodiment of the dancer's psychological impression, which, in turn, became the spectator's emotional reality. For Graham, the physical conflict centered on the interior conflict within the character represented by the dancer more than by his particular role performed or environment.

Philosopher Roger Garaudy chose to delineate three fundamental uses of rhythm and movement that, in turn, depicted three particular relationships between the choreographer and his

18

environment, expressed early in the twentieth century in the dance of Graham, Wigman, and Humphrey. In writing *Toute nouvelle période créatrice ...commence par une transgression ou une révolte*(Any new creative era...begins by either transgression or revolt),[17] Garaudy positioned dance as embodying *une manière totale de vivre le monde* (a total manner of living in the world).[18] Envisioned as a free-seeking element of popular culture, the dance of Maurice Bëjart became for Garaudy the legacy of modernism since it was within the modernist aesthetic that radical changes in how dance was viewed first appeared through description and interpretation.

Freedom and confinement, revolution and tradition were at odds in the early period of the twentieth century in the dance of Humphrey, Wigman, and Graham. These choreographers created seminal styles of expression encompassing non-traditional mergers of dance and music. Yet modernism in dance could not have occurred without prior reforms with form, color, and light by turn-of-the century choreographers Isadora Duncan and Loïe Fuller. Indirectly, the dances of Isadora Duncan grew out of her study of primitive cultures and performances, whereas Fuller's dance (discussed in the second chapter) sought to symbolically appeal to the senses through a fusion of color, shape, and lighting design.

Certainly Duncan's choreography, resplendent with graceful flowing movements of the arms chosen as imitations of Greek *bas reliefs*, influenced *Ballets Russes* choreographer Michel Fokine. Fokine, one of the century's foremost early ballet reformers, wrote in his manifesto the following set of rules designed to reject the canons of classical ballet, which had dominated the nineteenth century. These can be summarized as follows:

- Ready-made and established dance steps were not to be pre-formed but would be individually created as suited the dancing subject.

---

17 Garaudy, *Danser Sa Vie*, 95.
18 Ibid. 17.

- Dancing and mimetic gesture would have no meaning in a ballet unless they served as an expression of its dramatic action. They were not to be used as mere divertissement or entertainment.

- The new ballet admitted the use of conventional gestures only where required by the style of the ballet...and to replace gestures of the hands with a mimetic of the entire body.

- The new ballet refused to be the slave either of music or of scenic decoration. It recognized the alliance of the arts only on the condition of complete equality, allowing perfect freedom to both the scenic artist and to the musician.[19]

Fokine's challenge to the ominipotence of the classical dance, coupled with the emergence of the early, modern choreography for ballet initiated by Leonide Massine and by George Balanchine, would free ballet from late-nineteenth century classicism as expressed in such works as the three-act Tchaikowsky-Petipa collaborations: *The Nutcracker, Swan Lake,* and *The Sleeping Beauty.* These ballets, with their steps pre-formed to the subject and their emphasis on a prescribed series of *divertissements, soli,* and *pas de deux,* centered upon a prima ballerina and her cavalier. They were a far cry from such early *Ballets Russes* works Fokine would choreograph such as *Scheherezade* (1910) and *Les Sylphides* (1908), a ballet whose flowing arm movements are said to have been indirectly influenced by Fokine's first impressions of Isadora on her visit to the Imperial Ballet Theater in 1901. Not only did these latter two works utilize Fokine's reforms, they also represented a culmination of two movements: modernism in art and a contemporaneous breaking away from traditional ballet choreography.

    In his spectacle works initially conceived in the mid-twentieth century, Béjart departed from movement that used vocabulary from

---

19 From a letter to *The Times*, June 6, 1914. GBL Wilson, *A Dictionary of Ballet* (Harmondsworth; Penguin Books, 1957).

both traditions. His greatest inventiveness, however, is that of creative staging that traces its lineage to a semiology of multi-theatrical macrocosms. His use of the *métissage* principle, which, through its hybridness, emerges in performance as spontaneous spectacle and as "true" theater, are key to this inventiveness:

> I believe that the future of art lies in what we call in French, *métissage,* which is a racial mixture. It has always been a great civilization when many different races meet and make an explosion and something happens. The best example of this is in the United States. I believe in the mixing of voice, of singing, of theatrical qualities, and power.
>
> In the United States, you admit this when you present something you call musical comedy, but if it touches something else, you do not admit it. However, in my dances...some are pure dance, there are classical elements, modern elements, folklore...I think the vitality of my ballet comes from that. You can like it or dislike it but it is vital. [20]

In describing works of this early period, one might call Béjart a rebel, one whose art form intends to shock. His creativity consists of a fusion of *métissage,* or collage, of the elements that have marked him the strongest. As choreographer, his first works bearing the earmark of this rebellion were performed in post-World War II Paris. One of the most important, *La Symphonie pour un homme seul,* premiered one year after Martha Graham's company first appeared in Paris and two years following the premiere of Beckett's *Waiting for Godot.* Béjart's *La Symphonie pour un homme seul* is based on a similar theme of despair through a revolutionary use of repetition, sparseness of movement, and a vocabulary coupled with set designs which evoked, through lighting and props, the repetitiveness of everyday existence. Such basic onstage relationships as those of *décor* to scenic

---

20 Personal Interview: Maurice Béjart: 1975.

action, of onstage action to dialogue, and of lighting to movement and set design are key stylistic signatures that emerge from that period and remain throughout Béjart's artistic career. Unconsciously influenced by the *mise-en-scène* of the post-war theater, these early works are intricately timed and characterized by the earlier the *métissage* principle. Critical response to these earlier works was favorable, in part, because they related to what European audiences had seen previously in the theater and to the despair they understood in the period following World War II. Although often judged as "bad dance" by American critics, Béjart's ballets are rarely boring. At times they are uncomfortable to experience, yet nearly always they elicit emotional response from their audience.

Michel Polanyi refers to this highly emotional range or response as a process of "interiorization wherein we are allowed to know more than what we can actually tell about a given realm of knowledge." Polanyi's image is like that of a spectator at a sports event or an audience watching a theater performance. "Our body," states Polanyi in his text *The Tacit Dimension,*

> is the ultimate instrument of all our external knowledge... To interiorize is thus to identify ourselves (physically) with the teachings in question by making them function as the term of a tacit moral knowledge.[21]

To Polanyi, tacit knowing is knowing more than we actually tell, and it is to this sensation that we react when viewing a work by Béjart.

In Béjart's true or "virtual" theater, we face, not only in terms of the literary base of a work, but through its evolution as movement as well, the destruction and violation of form. Tacit knowing reminds us of what we know. It is the proper form of classical dance in its physical sense that we know, just as we read the "readerly text" of a given literary work. In their use of excessive sensuality and anti-classical postures, in their liberal displacement of key elements

---

21 Michel Polanyi, *The Tacit Dimension,* (New York: Doubleday, 1968), 72.

of a literary text through parody, through anti-classical posturing, or through other means, Béjart's images and movement forms make us uncomfortable because they destroy our preconceived knowledge of the formal codes of dance and of the familiar literary text. Still, while on one level there is destruction through choreography, on another there is a demand that we construct a different realm of knowledge.

Although violation of form exists, those very elements of *métissage* used by Béjart in this violation are skillfully woven into a context that is both purposeful and personal. Viewers must unconsciously interpret and react to two levels of destruction: that represented on the plane of movement and that of the literary masterpiece itself. Béjart is not classical and therefore his choreography has lacked the symmetrical beauty of a classically-formed Balanchine *corps de ballet* or the dark, dramatic impulse of Martha Graham. Nor is he strictly considered a company of dancers, although his dancers do, most of the time, perform *en pointe.*

When Béjart destroys, he re-forms, shaking our tacit awareness of original meaning. Often, literary forms whose meanings are transcendental reemerge revitalized to reflect upon the great questions of humanity. After undergoing this process of violation of form, no work appears the same, either in form or in meaning, as that of its parent work. Through this process of revolt, who may say what new and purer form may be derived?

A tri-partite subjective relationship between the choreographer and dancer-performer, between choreographer and audience, and between choreographer and dancer is the culmination of the process of *métissage.* As *metteur-en-scène,* whose presence is more or as important as actor-performer or as chosen literary text, Béjart defines both the dissemination of elements of the text and the dancer's function.

In the staging of *Cinq Nō modernes* for the Paris-based *Compagnie Rénaud-Barrault,* Béjart's rebellion against traditional text takes place through a fusing of contemporary stylistic elements onto the stage concept of Japan's highly ritualistic Nō drama. The result is a revolt of form that both extends and alters classical tenets of the form, such as its inherent physical postures and the movement and function of the chorus. The resultant staging, which will be discussed later in this chapter, challenges us to react more readily to the Nō play's subtle probing of an unseen past acting as cause to the present.

Similarly, in the spectacle performances of *Dichterliebe* (1978) and of *Notre Faust* (1981), through mises-en-scène designed to reflect sensual extremes, narratives emerge which are totally subsumed by the subjective preoccupations of the choreographer. The aim of this subjective involvement on the part of the choreographer is to engage the spectator, through correspondences of color, sound, and design, enabling participatation not only as spectator but as participant in the act of performance. Through multiple fusions of text with autobiography, through verbal text interspersed with danced performance, through lighting framed to text, and manipulation of props, multiple layers of meaning are instituted by Béjart. In *Dichterliebe*, these are juxtapositions of sensual extremes of color and sound montage that alternate between Schumann *lieder* and a Fellini film score composed by Nino Rota.

In *Notre Faust,* visual images dominate through opposition of textures of fabric, in the ornate brocade robes worn by the three archangels Michael, Gabriel, and Ezekiel. These contrast, in turn, with the basic black, white, and grey of background décor to constitute hidden codes. Juxtapositions are also present in the opposition of sound montage wherein such disparate elements as Argentinian tango and Bach mass alternate, and are arranged in conflicting partitions of sound. Because the code of *décor* in *Notre Faust* provokes tension with that of the sound montage (provoking a further "shock" between segments of literary text, enacted onstage), the spectator may choose to involve himself only with what he sees onstage and consequently to accept or reject Béjart's vision. It is precisely this imperative to react, to like or not like a particular staged performance, which causes it to emerge as both threatening and vital.

The first to fully advocate *métissage* as a principal and as affirmative means both to provoke and to sanctify was Antonin Artaud, whose theories of a "theater of cruelty" were made accessible to the French stage following World War II. Béjart's use of *métissage* is thus not new; nor was he the sole inventor of the principle of violation or destruction of a masterpiece. What is new is the way in which these principles were applied to the activity of danced performance.

In the "Second Manifesto of the Theater of Cruelty," the dramatist Artaud summons forth the vision of a theater in which the goal is to represent, "... the overlapping of images and movements [that) will culminate, through the collusion of objects, silences, shouts, and rhythms, or in a genuine physical language with signs, not words as its routes."[22] Béjart's theatrical imagery draws upon Artaud's concept of physical language to create dance that is much more than dance as an attitude or as lyrical complement to text. Béjart is instead concerned with elements of universal myth juxtaposed, subjectively, with his own concerns as director. In transposing his conceptions symbolically onto the stage by technical means or by movement forms, he parallels to the dramatic structure conceived by Artaud:

> For it must be understood that, in this quantity of movements and images arranged for a given length of time, we include both silence and rhythm as well as a certain physical vibration and commotion, composed of objects and gestures...made...and put to use. And it can be said that the spirit of the most ancient hieroglyphs will preside at the creation of this pure theatrical language. [23]

Principal among these parallels is Artaud's conception of solar and lunar dramatic form as the embracing of opposites. We can ask

---

22 Antonin Artaud,."The Theater of Cruelty (Second Manifesto*)" The Theater and Its Double.* (New York: Grove Press, 1958), 124.
23 Artaud, *The Theater and Its Double,* 62.

if the work of Béjart is to be considered solar in studying his focus on the explicit gesture of rebellion, or lunar being represented metaphorically by destruction of the literary text. Béjart's rebellious symbols often seem tilted in favor of negative values, creating a tension between what is tacitly present as text that is, in turn, redefined as affirmative gesture, and the lunar representation which extends beyond boundaries.

We will now examine in more detail how *métissage* is used as the formative principle in Béjart's creative stagings by examining more closely its uses in *Cinq Nō Modernes, Dichter*liebe, and in *Notre Faust*.

In "Notes en tours de Travail"[24] for the staging of *Cinq Nō modernes*, Béjart reveals affective affinities with Mishima the writer and alerts us that:

> ...la confession est un masque, l'apparence de la révélation, du dénudement qui est un artifice supreme de la sensibilité introvertie pour preserver son "moi" secret tout en faisant un pseudo étalage de confidences impudiques. [25]

> ...confession is a mask, the appearance of revelation, of laying bare as a supreme artifice of introverted sensitivity to preserve a secret self, all the while supplying a pseudo array of modest confidences

while revealing personal impressions of Mishima, the man, as,

> ..cet homme futur qui, ayant fait le tour desvanités brillantes du modernisme et ses mirages, plonge dans le passé impersonnel de la tradition véritable. [26]

---

24 Maurice Béjart. "Notes en cours de travail,." *Cinq Nō modernes* (Brussels, December, 1984).

25 Béjart. "Notes en cours de travail," 7.

26 Béjart. "Notes en cours de travail," 9.

> ...this man of the future who, having successfully run through the
> brilliant vanities of modernism and its mirages, plunges into the
> impersonal past of tradition.

caught in a revealing web of opposite extremes. Using as point of
departure the contemporary renderings by Yukio Mishima of the Nō
play, symbol of feudal Japan, Béjart explored in *Cinq Nō modernes*
a common aesthetic philosophy. In staging these plays for the
Compagnie Renaud-Barrault in Paris, he followed a movement
design that relied on the emotional perfection of the gesture, a
strategic device figuring in his choreography of more traditional
literary works. The severity or extremity of an angle of a given pose
traced not only the legitimacy or intensity of a given emotion, but also
its passage through time. The choreography of a given gesture,
(wherein stylized movement patterns performed in slow motion
alternate with frozen, static poses and indicate a character's present
actions), delineates the power of an affirmative, primary text which
is solar.

Conversely, dreamlike movement patterns functioned as
leitmotifs that define the psychology of characters such as Kayoko in
"Le Tambourin de Soie" (the silk tambourine) and La Vieille in
"Sotaba Komachi," indicating subtexts that are lunar, emotional
emblems. Within these plays, sequences of movement conceived
suggest hypnotic pacts, which in turn evoke traditional Nō
characters: the Waki and the Shite, who together command its chorus.
The interplay of theater conceived from a base of movement is
visualized through delicately profiled arching backs complemented
by subtle changes of direction performed in counterpoint, all causing
rebellion and dream to intermingle and merge as emblems.

For Béjart, the Nō served as a theatrical example of power rife
with layers of destruction. On a sparse stage framed by wooden
panels, the actor's skill is subtly likened to a martial art. In the modern
rendering of Nō by Béjart-Mishima, the traditional *mise-en-scène* of
the chorus and four musicians that sit at the foot of a long ramp
leading downstage is radically transformed. Using as point of

departure the life of the author and his reputed use of a personal army, Béjart dramatizes the text by dressing the chorus of actors as a corps of marching military cadets. Furthermore, and in an effort to destroy the presence of the chorus traditionally composed of men, Béjart introduces a single woman whose movements echo identically those of the men. A further level of destruction is attained through a chorus denied harsh make-up and deliberate voice changes demanded of the traditional Nō actor to impersonate women. To defy the transference of gender, traditionally evoked in Nō through masks and the presence of make-up, the role of a ninety-nine year old woman in the play "Sotaba Komachi" is performed unmasked.

It is in the creation of mood, however, that Béjart reveals Nō as a drama of meaningful silences. First, a single member of the chorus introduces a rhythm by a loud, sudden clapping of hands. Then he is joined by others as the rhythms become more complex. Finally, a counterpoint of three or four additional rhythms is introduced and is joined to the crisp foot patterns of marching cadets. Symbolic of the pride and spirit of military Japan the dance of the chorus reveals, at the same time, a subtext. The chorus speaks to its audience through these rhythms, which constantly change, forming oppositions to the silent gestures of individual actors.

In the representation of *Cinq Nō modernes*, dance is symbolical of text. In the play "Sotaba Komachi," the waltz the old woman performs symbolizes a past that her partner cannot remember. Thus, its performance serves as the principal action of the play. In "Lady Aoi," a series of movements suggesting somnambulic movements repeatedly alludes to the passage of time. The diversity of movement styles, ranging from traditional forms such as the waltz, to rigidly patterned military formations, suggests in Béjart's staging, the happenstance of boulevard theater. Whether contained in the rigorous march, or allowed to develop as slow somnambulic wanderings, movement is lunar, forming a subliminal screen that transcends the values of performance. For spectators who witness, the drama has a lunar effect on our senses, although it remains solar in its constant emphasis on destruction.

In *Dichterliebe*, choreographed in 1979, Béjart concerned himself with the artist as contemporary hero, beset with the dualism of good and evil. Extremes of sensuality are expressed, symbolically, through creative staging. To express the argument of modernism in *Dichterliebe*, which could be defined as a hierarchy of oppositions wherein the artist emerges victorious, Béjart made use of multiple layers of lighting, juxtapositions of sound, and a distinct relation of action to scenic space consisting of elements of cinematic montage framing sparse elements of décor.

In *Dichterliebe,* Béjart succeeded in taking the personal realm of the hero, represented by the dream, and proceeded to make universal symbols or archetypes of its images. As in many of his spectacle works, he relied on fragments of text, frequent set changes, elaborate costumes, and composition in the form of a collage. In the spectrum of works by Béjart that have been chosen here, as exampled by which Béjart may be catagorized, *Dichterliebe* proceeds from the literary to the personal. The artist poured out stream-of-consciousness images and sequences of dream that, although illogical, reveal a penchant for a fusion of opposite symbols.

In Béjart's seminal works of this period, archetypal images were formed that may be fused together, held separately, or interchanged while still maintaining a viable representation, allowing for a maximum level of decodability. Considered by Béjart himself as "a very natural ballet," *Dichterliebe* began as an inspiration for the creation of a work to the music of Schumann. He stated in an interview, "So I began to work. Then I thought of a second work to music used by Fellini, so I asked the composer, Nino Rota, (who is my friend) to create a score." [27]

In what he claimed to be his first "natural ballet," Béjart handles his images wildly. Characters appear, reappear, interact, and

---

27 Interview: Maurice Béjart, Brussels, 1978.

fade as they are replaced by others. Complete images shift in flowing patterns as quickly as do single characters. Once again, Béjart destroys on three levels: in his décor where visual images initiated by dream at one moment "burst" through stage backdrops to represent a transcendance or "going beyond" the frame, (or, in a Derridean sense, transcendance of boundary); in his movement, through interspersion of clashing dance styles ranging from Argentinian tango to steps from a conventional *barre;* and, in his blending of sound as when the Schumann score mingles with tunes of Italian composer, Nino Rota. All resound by working together in a synthesis destined to transcend traditional formats of the stage.

Inherent "devices" of destruction are apparent in the first scene where the Hero, performed by solo dancer Jorge Donn enters the stage center. Isolated, the dancer pauses before commencing to perform a sedately classical solo composed entirely of adagio sequences and steps performed *à terre*. First, he measures the opening phrases of steps, executing *tendu battements* in silence; then he repeats the same sequence of steps to the Schumann melody. As he dances, three ballerinas in simple pink leotards perform at the barre that frames the stage. It is interesting to note that in Béjart's particular use of *métissage,* the ballet codes an *écriture* of classicism and conformity, even while "writing" into its staging elements of destruction.[28] The accompanying three dancers may be understood to represent the three graces, who accompany the young god they follow. Against the stillness, a voice speaks the following verse illustrating Béjart's predilection for the primacy of speech as an element of performativity.

> Life has but one risk,
> But what, if one does not care,
> If one wins or loses?

---

28 In many of Béjart's works of this period, the function of the ballet *danseur* is symbolically represented on stage apart from its performative function, thoroughly delineated by the framing device of the barre.

Following this utterance, the image changes, becoming complex. Two figures enter to join the poet. They are a Woman dressed in White accompanied by a man (conversely, in Black) who function as archetypes of light and darkness. As the Man in Black sits at the poet's desk, a point of view is established from which the audience may in turn serve as an unseen witness to the devices of theatricality. As the Hero-poet begins to waltz with the Woman in White a loudspeaker blares, *Mais attention!* (May we have your attention!). The meaning is clear: in dreams, all is the opposite of what it seems. The darkly-lit stage, juxtaposed against the dancing figures, underscores the inherent duality or representation.   Yet another dimension of truth in representation extends to the character: the Woman in White is really a man, a deception of which only the audience is aware.

Enter dancer Rita Poelvoorde as the Young Girl in Pink. Dressed entirely in pink, except for a long black cape, she listens to a second voice:

> Solitude, since my childhood;
> solitude, despite my family and friends,
>   But...I NEED LIFE!

The spectator may never be quite sure what the texts mean, yet he is allowed freedom to create meaning from their presences. Through his displacement of the text, Béjart draws his audience surreptitiously toward the image of the performance.

In the next scene, the Hero waltzes with the Young Girl in Pink and is observed by the figure of the horse, Pegasus, who enters stage left to stare at the Man in Black. Hardly ten minutes of performance pass before Béjart tries once again to delude his audience. If Black is symbol of evil, the young girl's cloak is a warning and, thus, forms a parallel to the image of the Woman in White.

As the poet tries to free himself from his dreams, he experiences Pegasus who, while wrestling with the Man in Black, tosses and turns as though in a nightmare. Then, on the backdrop provided by the stage, Béjart projects the image of a modern city where huge toy building blocks are placed onstage and inscribe, in bold script, the letters *L I E B E*. As successive layers of meaning inherent in the performance become apparent, the distinction between the various levels of representation inherent in *Dichterliebe* becomes more and more complex. In the succeeding scene, an anonymous character appears, interacts with a companion, leaves the stage, and reappears. At each successive reappearance, color marks the psychology of the relationship between the character and the elements of mise-en-scène. Character, in *Dichterliebe*, becomes symbol, to which are ascribed a further dimension of dark and light. This narrative ascribing, through color nuances, of the relation of good dreams to bad, or of truth to falsehood, imples an ever-threatening struggle.

If *Liebe* is Béjart's culminating image of idealism and good, the Motorcycle Angel completes the juxtaposition of binary opposites onstage through representations of evil and the covert. The strongest emotional scene occurs when the protective dimension of reality, symbolized by the dance itself, as an encadrement of barres, is broken amid shrieking whistles of an impending visit by police to rid "the stage" of the angel and his dark companions. Except for the small white flares of threatening headlamps the stage is dark. In a gesture symbolizing both sponteneity and shock, the Angel rips apart the backdrop. As wooden *barres* break, parameters of representation are threatened, leaving the stage in chaos. The metaphor is at times unclear or even undecipherable, a multi-layered symbol conceived as a system of binary oppositions which exceed the boundaries of representation. In this act of destruction, the audience confronts the element of surprise or shock. The audience's resultant tacit response or audible rejection of the staged images is encouraged as cinematic projections ranging from chess sets to procelain dolls make visible one more layer of reality.

Derived as devices of cinematic projection, these props even more effectively juxtapose with the leitmotif of a specific character. Thus, the chess set extends the symbol of the Hero who wrestles, in a following scene, with a Football Quarterback to symbolize the opposition of the banal to the ethereal. The Quarterback attempts to carry away the ballerinas; conversely, they appear lifeless as porcelain dolls and seem to oppose the freshness and innocence suggested by the Young Girl in Pink. Each staged frame initiated by successive *enchainments* of movement invites endless interpretations, yet it is precisely the element of endless choice coupled with that of surprise which causes us not only to witness, but to experience this work as an attempt at conscious control.

Yet another layer of interpretation in *Dichterliebe* is possible through the symbolization of color. In addition to a character's association with a particular symbol, he is also assigned a leitmotif of color and sound through which a particular subliminal meaning is ascribed. Movement as signature guides Béjart's choreography for this work causing it to become coded, thus forming a counterpart to the academic rigidity of performance. As the Young Girl in Pink performs the steps of ballet's academic vocabulary, embodying a series of *bourrées* followed by *piqué* turns, the Hero performs the same basic steps *à terre* at stage left. Yet another dimension of *métissage* allying the literary to the performative is conceived as the character symbolizing Woman in Red appears accompanied by a second dancer, in drag, representing George Sand. As the two pose centerstage, two other dancers appear who perform certain starkly angular movement patterns enhanced by the declamation of verbal texts.

Dancer Angèle Albrecht then appears as a pregnant mother who, allied to the characterization of The Woman in Red, shouts in German, a line from Walther von der Vogelweider, *im wunderschonen monat mai* (In the merry month of May) suggesting multiple interpretations of sensuality and the opposition of the literal to the real. In a shrill, commanding voice she shrieks and does not dance, but engulfs the Hero in a bright red maternity dress.

As a performer creating a "staging within a staging", dancer Catherine Verneuil enacts the character of George Sand through a series of twists, struts, and the arcane performance of a charleston. Carrying a microphone, Verneuil assumes the roles of interlocutress and mistress of ceremonies as she chants, in a different rhythmic sequence from that of Albrecht, the following text:

> George Sand, George Sand, is one of those aging ingenues who
> never want to quit the stage;
> She is Stupid,
> She is Heavy,
> ....and she talks too much!

Such characterizations as those of the Woman in Red and of George Sand may be referred to as static. They are depicted through limited movement, performed repetitively, yet sparingly; Béjart creates specific attitudes through his characters that function as emblems beyond their presence as performers. By thus extending this presence to encompass the symbolic, he causes them to mirror ironically the duplicity inherent in our own values.

In this work Béjart calls upon a process described by Jacques Derrida in his essay, *La Clôture de la représentation.* For Derrida, as for Artaud, the theater becomes the primordial, privileged sight of destruction and of imitation. Thus, the theater's function is to dissociate or destroy, or to extend beyond the boundaries of its own "theatrical" form, or architecture. Thus, what is enacted onstage extends beyond the boundary of mere representation. For these critics, theater must do so if it is to realize its full significance as an act of cruelty.[29]

Responding to emotions aroused by dual appearances of the Woman in Red and George Sand, the poet shouts to the audience

---

29 Jacques Derrida. "La Clôture de la Representation," *L'Ecriture et la différence* (Paris: Seuil, 1967), 345.

"NO," a gesture echoed by absolute silence.   By establishing a negative point of view the poet's wielding of the power of closure brings into play again the dual fusion of reality and dream onstage. In the next scene, the character who symbolizes the Football Star reappears to alert the spectator to what Béjart conceives as the banality of the present moment associated with the aftermath of the experience of modernity.   As he makes a formation with his team, they exit, carrying on their backs the ballerinas, so as to suggest the dominion of the real over the ethereal. Simultaneous to the appearance of this image, a skull, symbolizing death, is placed to the left of the poet's desk requiring a spatial restructuring of scenic space implying both characterization and the representation of its scenic opposite. Throughout the work's succession of frames, a single character is referenced through stage action that establishes a dialogue of gestures defining frames of narrative.   In turn, these actions alternate with scenes wherein a given character enters the blurred region of the boundary of representation, identifying with the spectator and establishing point of view.

Béjart employs comically other symbols such as one wherein dancer Bertrand Pie appears as a Cat who gestures frantically before offering the microphone to George Sand. Yet another occurs when a group of clowns perform a series of *fouetté* turns after waltzing with the poet, whose labor they try to distract.   Meanwhile, in another area of the stage, the character referred to as the Man in Black assumes a role as interlocuteur. In *Dichterliebe,* Béjart's insistence that the stage function as a macrocosm of dream symbols and oppositions opens his danced theater to innumerable interpretations.

In contrast, Béjart states of *Notre Faust* that:

C'est un ballet qui corréspond à moi, actuellement, mais qui est en même temps presqu'un ballet d'enfance. J'ai parfois l'impression que c'est mon premier ballet...que ce soit par le style, par la façon de raconter, par la façon d'être...je ne l'ai pas du tout ressenti en le faisant, en le construisant...mais, la veille de la générale, j'ai eu l'impression que ça me rappelait *Orphée*, mon premier ballet-soirée. En effet, il y a la même force et la même naiveté, le même espace cosmique les mêmes défauts peut-être...réellement, *Notre Faust* me rappelle fort cette époque! [30]

It's a ballet which suits me; actually, but at the same time it's almost a ballet of childhood. Sometimes I feel it's my first ballet, whether through style, through the manner of its telling...I didn't sense this in creating or assembling its elements...but the evening of the dress rehearsal, I had the impression so that it caused me to remember *Orpheus*, my first full-length evening spectacle. There's the same force and innocence, the same cosmic space, even the same faults ...truly, *Notre Faust* recalls this time period.

Béjart refers to *Notre Faust* as "a first ballet." He considers that it embodies a signature for his style. In this work, as in each of his works which utilize the principle of *métissage*, he begins with a single structure derived from the archetypal narrative to use as a base. Secondly, he gives to a solo dancer a principal place onstage and a power to guide and to wield its energy through various shiftings of prop and other elements of stage design. Finally, by meshing dance performance with stage design, he imposes on performance a layer of autobiography. By this imposition he proceeds to recreate and, at the same time, destroy the audience's conception of the literary form as it has previously been known.

Viewing the work gives rise to many questions concerning Bejart's intended use of musical collage as a dramatic element. Conceived as a sung mass (an idea adopted from Goethe), *Notre Faust* begins with a scene in heaven where all participants are Angels, the Holy Virgin, or Saints. Like baroque art, it displays an aesthetic that is not centered, but that departs from various points, in tension, toward an undefined position of equilibrium. Within this work three

---

30 Antoine Livio, "Plein Feu sur Maurice Béjart," *Dance Perspective* (Paris: February, 1967): 12.

distinct levels of sound alternate with silence throughout its three-hour performance: tangos, Dixieland jazz, and musical partitions of the *Bach Mass in B minor.*

Béjart reveals elements of his chosen masterwork and assembles these subjectively, whether in his choice of *décor,* music, or text. "I chose the Bach Mass," he relates, "because Goethe was born in the same year Bach died. And the first time that Mass was ever played was after Bach's death. Bach fought with Mendelssohn, his friend, to have that Mass played! And that is why I chose that special work."[31]

In *Notre Faust,* Béjart reveals the creation of the central character, Mephistopheles through the symbolic use of masks to reveal psychological traits. Masks create parody more in the female roles of Helen, Marguerite, and the Mother than in male roles. Appearing to Faust in masks that serve to convey a dual personality, the dancers' performances represent the destruction of Faust's ideal of womanhood. Through the device of the mask, the Mother appears overly maternal. Later, her characterization changes and she becomes possessive. In similar manner, madness of Marguerite is portrayed as becoming guilefully mischievous; and Helen of Troy is allowed multiple metamorphoses onstage as a vamp. Although male characters wear masks, they do not constitute projections of character. In one instance, Mephistopheles dons the mask of Marguerite, suggesting that the root of his cunning is transferred to one of the three feminine images. Onstage, this action is not only suggested, but is also made apparent by constant shifting of *décor* indicating fluctuations of mood. Thus, Béjart would seem to tell us, through symbolic uses of mask, that women become complex, mad creatures, and men, by being subjected to the woman's complexity, assume responsibility for evils the woman may commit. Like the protagonist, Faust, the chorus appears in black. The only character in white is

31 Norma McLain Stoop, Interview Maurice Béjart, *Dance Magazine* (New York, 1977).

Mephistopheles, introducing to the dramatic structure yet another dimension, that of the absurd.

In the representation of *Notre Faust*, Béjart uses Goethe's narrative as linear plot construction on which to apply various forms of destruction. The first of these is the juxtaposition of costumed character against skillfully manipulated text fragments. Here Béjart makes particular use of feminine symbols that he parodies with masks which serve as weapons of disguise. The figures of Faust are represented by doubles: of Faust as a middle-aged man and of Faust as a youth. The double, in contrast to the masked characters, creates illusive ambiguity.

Of interest in *Notre Faust* is the interspersing of imagined personal scenes within the narrative structure. One example occurs when the little boy Faust, accompanied by his mother, turns cartwheels beside the sea. Another concerns the absurd interspersion of the music hall tap-dance routine *The Lullaby of Birdland* into the scene depicting *Walpurgisnacht*.

These different applications of destruction are at the base of Béjart's creativity and are a means through which various aspects of the narrative are disassociated. Yet, beyond the juxtaposition of *décor*, Béjart introduces several scenes from his own childhood in the second act, adding to the already multi-layered system of codes that of autobiography. In these scenes, a mother returns from a ball wearing a long white dress to see her little boy playing gaily in his sailor suit while merrily turning cartwheels. The city, of course, is Marseilles and the little boy is Béjart. In an interview, Béjart explained that:

> these are personal memories of my mother....because my mother died when I was seven. Then, when I made this ballet, I found that Goethe's second *Faust* was preoccupied by the subject of mothers. Of course, I was born on the seaside, and a memory of

38

my mother always goes with the souvenir of the sea, because the
sea is the mother of life. [32]

Voice is effectively used in *Notre Faust* to provide additional
variations and becomes a dramatic realm wherein Béjart, by altering
its internal structure, achieves even greater unity with danced
movement on both visual and metaphysical planes. As the character
Marguerite becomes insane, she begins to babble incessantly in
German, causing the use of a particular language to affect a grotesque
magnification of character that, in turn, forces audience response.
This representation of madness is partly influenced by the
juxtaposition of language for language's sake. Marguerite's
mumblings represent incoherent babblings through text spoken by
Béjart himself, through a loudspeaker. Dressed in black, the
loudspeaker is made to visible through the presence of a single red
cord attached to the stage, giving to the montage of sounds the
controlling element of spectacle.

> In the Beginning was the word,
> In the Beginning was the thought,
> In the Beginning was the force.

is the initial verbal text spoken by Béjart himself as interlocuteur in
the opening scene. Sound becomes a foil that not only enhances the
image but also undermines it. Thus, a tension occurs between
narrative and acoustic frames of the tableau. One instance of this
tension occurs when Mephistopheles, wearing the mask of
Marguerite, performs a tango with Faust. Here, even the choice of the
dance, the tango, becomes an important element of destruction and
hence of interpretation.

Developed through ornate contrasts of *décor* and glaring
contrasts of color, image, and sound, the spectacle work *Notre Faust*
reveals much of Béjart. In the ballet, Faust has access to a personal

---

32 Personal Interview: Maurice Béjart, 1975.

mirror through which he is able to gain redemption. The only possible escape for Faust is revealed in the spoken text, wherein Goethe/Faust states:

> J'ai appris la philosophie, la médecine
> le droit et malheureusement la théologie.

> I have learned philosophy, medicine, law,
> and unhappily, theology.

a text which may be compared with the more personal tone of Béjart, used as part of the sound montage:

> Il nous reste à faire le dernier voyage
> Au fond de la mémoire.
> Je possède la clef d'argent.
> Au commencement était la mère.

> It remains for us to make the final voyage
> to the depth of memory.
> I possess the silver key.
> In the beginning was the mother.

Speech is used minimally by Béjart to probe the pscyhology of Faust. As in Goethe's tale, where Faust must struggle to distinguish good from evil, Béjart has his personal Faust select from two German texts written on the two blackboards that are placed on either side of the stage. *Die Sterben* (the death) thus opposes *Die Tat* (the deed) leaving in balance for the spectator an alluring logic of anxiety and suspension in time..

By sharing in the process of destroying a single masterpiece wherein images may be imagined, yet are unseen, the audience may participate in a continous process of destruction and of recreation. As modernist archetypes, *Dichterliebe* and *Notre Faust* thus offer formative elements inscribed sensually through language and visual images. These images remind us tacitly not only of the archetype itself, but also its possibilities for destruction, and for redemption. Through the staging of *Notre Faust* and other works of this period, the archetype is rendered personal as an emblem of modernist choreography.

Through these choreographies, Béjart screens all elements of staging to allow a controlled spontaneity to emerge as choreography. Coupling processes of *métissage* in staging with themes based on rebellion, Béjart's interplay of destruction and redemption achieves a humor which is at once compatible with that applied by Artaud to theater. An example of this dynamic in *Notre Faust* occurs when Mephistopheles tries to destroy Faust's sense of good and evil. Male dancers wearing black gloves and dressed in drag perform a can-can to "The Lulluby of Broadway" while, simultaneously, Faust performs to movements of an Argentine tango. Faust's indecisiveness is conveyed through his choice of partner: he does not choose Marguerite, nor Helen, nor his mother, but instead Mephistopheles himself.

Faust, the hero, must choose between multiple selves that are depicted as double images; for example, he must attempt to distinguish between good and evil, the first fruit of an errant imagination. In summary, the principal stage action of the tragic revealed through comic means, through multiple juxtapositions of verbal text, through movement, or through sound, all directly reclaim a space wherein the spectator engages tacitly in processes of performance.

In these three seminal works: *Cinq Nō modernes, Dichterliebe,* and *Notre Faust,* distinctive characteristics of a uniquely personal style emerge as projection, as distortion, or as description of a literary archetype. In their respective stagings, Béjart effectively controls textual layers. In the area of color, black, white, and grey function as a means of background control on which to project diverse textures; in the area of staging, lighting corresponds to frames of meaning. In the area of sound, he juxtaposes and merges sections of verbal text. Finally, in the area of movement, classical, modern, and popular styles are mixed. Common everyday objects for Béjart become symbols of the mystical or an embodiment of aspects of the terrible emerge as supplements. Within the parameters of these case studies, Béjart may be considered either as choreographer and *metteur-en-scène* or as performer, simply because the dances he creates manifest, to a large degree, elements of his own subjectivity.

It has been said there is no "new"art; thus the tradition of modernism to which Béjart belongs is neither derived from classicism nor from prior modernist currents. Rather, his ballet of the decades of the seventies and eighties can be considered as a hybrid form that offers an alternative tradition for dance. Thus, in Béjart's creative ballet, we can perceive an ancestry of cross-hatchings between two arts, of dance and of theater, wherein innovations in each impact the other decisively. Béjart's values may be defined by and traced to the fusion of forms that began in the theater of the late-nineteenth century by early pioneers of modern dance and by choreographers such as Fokine.

This study places emphasis on preceding systems wherein violation of form constitutes a seminal act of revolt leading toward a newer, more powerful, use of the stage. In the case of Béjart, the creator's personal idealism subsumes the literary text, resulting in an intentional and emotional approach to danced performance.

CHAPTER TWO
THE SACRED DANCE AS SYMBOLISM:
HISTORICAL ANTECEDENTS

In this chapter questions of form *in mises-en-scène* used by Béjart in his several ballets are considered in light of their historic and aesthetic antecedents. How the ballets appear onstage, the stylistic signatures with which they are linked in relation to decorative embellishments and sound accompaniments raise aesthetic issues which cause us to recall earlier theatrical systems, in particular late-nineteenth century attempts by symbolist poets to emphasize a total staging reliant on movement to create a particular mood or dominant symbol.

This language of the body defies expectation because it precedes rational consciousness:

> Il faut que la connaissance rationelle ne soit pas le premier mot des mots. La subordination classique du langage à la pensée et du corps au langage.[33]

> It is necessary that rational knowledge not be the first word of all words. The classical subordination of language to thought and of the body to language.

In his doctrine of *corréspondances,* Baudelaire perceived a supernatural realm inspired and seen by an artist aspiring to priest-like purity:

> La nature est un temple où de vivants piliers
> Laissent parfois passer de confuses paroles;
> L'homme y passe à travers des forêts de symboles
> Qui l'observent avec des regards familiers.[34]

---

33 Jacques Derrida, *L'Ecriture et la différence*, (Paris: Seuil, 1977), 341.
34 Charles Baudelaire, quoted in *Poètes Symbolistes*, ed. S. Braak, (Amsterdam: S.L. Van Looy, 1924), 11.

> Nature is a temple where living pillars
> Often let confused words pass.
> Man passes there through forests of symbols
> Who observe him with familiar glances.

Although the artist's activity is not a part of this realm, he is constantly exposed to its extremes: the ambivalence between the purity to which he aspires and the temptations of the world to which he is continuously exposed are constantly present in Baudelaire's poetry.

For Baudelaire, the world of the senses possessed a natural translation into terms which corresponded to feelings and ideas. By analogy to all of the senses, the relationship of the mind of the artist to the natural objects he perceived lay at the base of the poet's essential doctrine. Stating that colors, sounds, and smells were unified, spiritually, into one teleologic experience, Baudelaire, in the last verses of his poem, alludes to a synaesthetic interrelating of senses that causes them to achieve a higher level of awareness and stimulate the spirit. Thus, according to the degree to which a viewer participates in what occurs on the stage, he is also a receiver of sensual stimuli, a participant in his own awakening or experience of shock. According to the degree of this participation, he is a visionary or "seer" of a work of art.

Through significant influence of Baudelaire, the role of the artist as observer of inner life emerged. The artist, who at the same time was endowed with a kaleidoscopic consciousness, moved in rhythm with life's deepest pulsations, and constantly experienced the tension between the satanic and the divine. Often he felt the extremes of sensualism set against spiritual ideals.

No less important than Baudelaire's vision as artist were his beliefs about theatrical form itself. Baudelaire imagined actors on stilts and wearing masks which were more expressive than the human face. He also envisioned performers who mouthed their lines with loudspeakers or, through the use of doubles, interpreted their roles.

Women would be played by men, evoking a parody. In his critical text *Sur Mon Coeur mis à nu*, he writes, "Of my opinions on the theater, that which I have always found to be the most beautiful...is the luster, a beautiful luminous crystal object; complex, circular, symmetrical."[35] From German idealism, and from the aesthetic theories of Richard Wagner in particular, the Symbolists gained the ability to view the world idealistically and to engage in a significant freedom of experimentation in introducing inventions to the stage. Their experimentation gleaned influences from the fields of science and philosophy, from occultism, and from Scandinavian plays, such as the controversial late-nineteenth century works of Henrik Ibsen, translated for the French stage.

As innovators, the Symbolist poets undertook the task of challenging assumptions about the nature of a work of art and the duties of the artist to the genre in which the work was expressed. The Symbolists broke with established stage form and admired especially those artists, such as German composer, Richard Wagner, who had suffered for the sake of their art. Inspired by the composer's creation of irregular rhythms and musical cadences for the stage, they sympathized with Wagner, whom detractors at the Paris Opera hissed at following the failure of the *première* of the opera, *Tannhauser*.[36] Each Symbolist poet peopled his art with his own personal symbols and ignored his critics, with Wagner, the originator of the *gesamtkunstwerk*, (often subtitled in his writings as "a theater of the future"), as his inspiration.

By the late 1890s, rampant experimentation in the performance of literary texts by Symbolist poets who had followed the principles of Wagner, would result in an anarchy for the stage liberating other art forms. Its legacy of influences would include not

---

35 Baudelaire, *Sur mon coeur mis à nu*. trans: J.J. Marchande "Crayoné au Théâtre." (Paris: L'Herne, 1970), 82.
36 Richard Wagner's *Tannhauser* premiered in Paris in 1861. The opera failed to meet with critical acclaim due to the audacity of the *bacchanale* preluding the opera's first act.

only the modernist dance of Loïe Fuller, but also the newly-formed *Ballets Russes* company of Sergei di Diaghilev.

Analogous to the intent to project beyond the frame of staged representation, Symbolist poets sought to portray, on their sparse stages, realities that existed "beyond" the dimension of performance. Their creations comprised what might ordinarily be termed poetic representation. Frequently, an object construed verbally could coexist with the paradox of its "staged" absence, symbolized in performance by the placing and displacing of objects, effecting an interplay of substitutions as a continuous process of representation.

Wagner's ideal of a "total"art work, (in which theater was used as an intersection of all forms toward a common form,) stemmed in part from the composer's desire to recover the totality of art which the Renaissance had sought to recover from ancient Greece. This ideal union presupposed the existence of a trinity of poetry, music, and mimed action to which would be added architecture and painting. This theory was not without precedent, yet Wagner was the first to develop theoretically the idea of a total art form into a complete theatrical system. The inconsistencies that would later become apparent between the staging theories of Wagner and their application were based, in part, on a discrepancy between the desire for a grandiose architecture for his theater, (as a stage for actors whose statures depicted almost superhuman characters) and the simplistically conceived principle of theatrical *décor*.

Inconsistencies between Wagner's principles and their application, and their re-application by the symbolists were most evident in principles governing *décor*. For example, in one production, the forest where the hero Siegfried kills the dragon was designed as a mere group of branches clinging together in a kind of romantic imagery. Medieval architecture was likewise carefully reproduced as a flat castle motif.

Late-nineteenth century painters were as yet unable to conceive of a *décor* principle equal in power to the cadre of mythology conceived by Wagner for opera. It was the need for a such a principle to embody the mythic design envisioned by the composer that initially spurred experimentation in stage designs among young Symbolist poets. The attack on the senses of the largely working class audience of late nineteenth-century Paris was often achieved through décors where painting, perfumed aura, and costumes of nebulous gauze illumined the stage, under the spell of a poetry whose resplendent musical power lay in the strophe. Yet, if the music and theory of Wagner had left its imprint on the Symbolist poet, the envisioning of an intermediary figure designed to act as a go-between between actor and audience also influenced the staging of their plays. This idea would lead to the later role of the stage-director as overseer of the staged conception of an artistic work, brought forth in Symbolist theaters by poet-directors who undertook multiple experiments in *synaesthesia* or the synthesis of artistic genres into corresponding effects of the senses involving color, scent, and audial representations of narrative elements. As creators of works that they also performed, the presence of the poet-director was condemned by critics, but lauded in innumerable small reviews that were also self-published. If their productions enlightened viewers in creating an audience largely of working class spectators, they also attracted among their diverse viewers a radical public populated by youth disenchanted by France's defeat in the Franco-Prussian War.

We can ask why the subjective presence of creator-performer appealed onstage to an audience composed not only of working class patrons eager to experience the fruits of anarchy, but also to admirers and patrons from all levels of society anxious to visualize radical change in theatrical mannerisms. The appeal of these plays depended on the interplay of symbols meant to stir the audience to participate and to instill in them a sense of awe, as though viewing a mirror-image through which to stimulate a like creative process.

Such arrays of symbols, although sometimes banal, nevertheless marked the beginnings of revolutionary theatrical forms practiced over a century ago. In such venues as the *Théâtre Libre*[37] of Antoine, the *Théâtre de l'Oeuvre* of Lugné-Poe,[38] and the *Théâtre d'Art* of Paul Fort[39] to give but two examples, artists experimented with such elements as Wagner's principle of *leitmotif*[40] applying it to word sounds and to forms. Poets would group a series of words or gestures into readable symbols that translated into a series of codes for the stage. The highly individual plays which resulted corresponded to the poet's own psyche and scheme of ideas.

Although critics of the period panned those plays whose meanings were too idiosyncratic to be understood or leaned toward narcissism, the big debate seemed to lay in their authenticity as theater. Were these productions artistic works of the stage or a mish-mash of experimentation undertaken by amateurs trying to transform a Wagnerian arts synthesis based on myth into a personal equation? Lamentably, simplistic symbols that confused the public and that often conveyed a message no more significant than "life is very mysterious" were sprinkled among the Symbolist theater's more profound aspirations. Although these theaters survived, if only to serve as transitions toward future movements, the poets involved aimed to express a total artistic freedom and did so by upsetting all previously given assumptions about the theater. For the Symbolists, inspired by Baudelaire and by Wagner, art proceeded from the divine. In 1892, a critic wrote:

> The Symbolist theater, more modern and of a higher truth than
> that of the realist drama, is the theater of the future; for it is the

---

37 The *Théâtre Libre* of Antoine performed in Paris sporadically between 1887 and 1893.
38 The *Théâtre de l'Oeuvre* of Aurélian Lugné-Poë inspired a more stable idealism than did the *Théâtre d'Art* of Paul Fort.
39 From November, 1890 to March, 1892 the *Théâtre d'Art* presented a series of seven programs in Paris.
40 A short theme or musical idea consistently associated with a character, a place, or an object.

only theater to provoke the sacred tremor which only divine art
gives. [41]

The Symbolist theater included among the many principles of its
mise-en-scène the representation of a particular symbol to evoke
meaning beyond an image shape, color, or shifting physical forms.
Often this symbol grew out of an arbitrary judgment on a spiritual
state. Nevertheless the innovations that occurred lasted and served as
transitions to future art forms. In making abundant use of Baudelaire's
doctrine of correspondances (a sound could suggest a color, a color
suggest an idea of melody and their combination could translate into
specific ideas), the Symbolists attempted to assimilate all art forms
under the emblem of one vast symbol.[42]

Their anarchic stagings often met with unfavorable reviews
on the part of the critic who interpreted these plays as consisting of
too many symbols, of being too subjective, or of trying to evoke an
overly literary meaning through the overuse of particular methods of
staging. The substance of the reviews of these early plays may be
paraphrased as follows: in the theater of the Symbolists, the manner
in which various stage elements were used to delineate a symbol
distinguished the performance of text from spoken discourse through
the forming of multiple codes. In addition, costumes of light gauze,
subtle changes in sound shifting from whispers to poetic text to prose,
and static movement constructions based on a single gesture all
blended to convey a particular *attitude*. In this theater, static auditory
segments of sound effected through the utterance of incoherent
speech, intended a separate level of sense perception and meaning.
Often the ensemble of special fragmented effects of sound and
movement was confusing.

It seems obvious that Béjart's use of the *metteur-en-scène* as
performer and his particular arrangement of onstage elements to
represent a system of subjective-expressive representation could be

---

41 F. Coulon, *L'Art Littéraire*, (Paris: October, 1892).
42 *Les Poètes Symbolistes*, ed. Braak, 19.

viewed as a text resplendent of late-nineteenth century essays in Symbolism, serving as a transition to more solidly construed multi-theatrical macrocosms as discussed in Chapter One. In comparing Symbolist arrangements of stage elements to particular groupings used in Béjart's works of the mid-seventies, one recalls the insightful review by *New York Times* critic Jack Anderson:

> ...his choreography consists of short phrases of fragmentary movements. These suffice to indicate the dancers' apartness, but together their elements have no lyrical flow. Togetherness was not made all that...different from isolation. However, because Mr. Béjart can devise striking gestures and poses, many of these movement fragments were pictorially effective.[43]

The validity of "pictorial effectiveness" in Béjart's work was but one problem advanced by critics such as Anderson in the late-seventies. Pictorial "effectiveness" mainly derived from form, from terse steps that connected sequences linked to meaning only when Béjart so desired, and that can be compared to the symbolist use of "static" poses in profile. "Character" in Béjart's contemporary stagings may also be indicated by a single pose, such as when the Rose of the Desert in *Golestan*, performed by Suzanne Farrell, arches her back while pressing a single forward battement. Likewise, the movement of the predator-female in *La Symphonie pour un homme seul* emphasizes, through the pose where the female swings her legs back and forward over the male, an isolated, predatory posture. In each work, static movement affords the audience a single moment of recognition through which a pose may be construed or presented as symbol of narration. In contrast, the inevitable contradiction of Béjart's choreography occurs when a series of poses is linked as an arbitrary system of signs that, through their separateness, connect allegorically to suggest even deeper personal meanings.

---

43 Jack Anderson, "Ballet: Béjart's *Verdi,*" *The New York Times*, March 1979.

These personal meanings enact a subjective sphere through which the viewer is able to decode in each spectacle an autobiographical gesture or narrative. Thus Béjart assigns to a given work a symbolism that is subjective, yet through which a given ballet presupposes a deliberate methodology. The subjectivity of Béjart's ballets are both strength and weakness and may be allied to criticisms of late nineteenth century symbolist stagings. With regard to audience reception and understanding this subjectivity posed a problem to late nineteenth-century critics. Certainly the inherent subjectivity of many of the plays by the Belgian poet Maurice Maeterlinck and others, and the serious attitude of their poet-creators resulted in confusing meanings for the spectator. After all, a single actor could not evoke the entire complexity of a poetic metaphor all alone. On one plane, courage to innovate, on another, poor reviews, pointed the way to the demise of the Symbolist theater. Confusion toward symbols, and uncertainty about what a playwright "really meant" is evident in a review of *L'Intruse* by Belgian playwright Maurice Maeterlinck:

> In *L'Intruse*, a woman is dying while, in the next room, her relatives gather. They try to break the silence with brief bits of conversation until an invisible stranger enters their midst. He is seen by one of the guests, a blind grandfather who, as the stranger enters, traces the sign of the cross. As the grandfather is making this gesture, a man from the adjoining room announces the woman has died. The deliberate ambiguity of the symbol of blindness appears in *L'Intruse*. No one knew what Maeterlinck meant to convey by this symbol except that he clearly intended it to be one. [44]

The problem of this theater is thus one of decipherment or of transformation of meaning in text to methods of staging. At times, in order that we as spectators have a more acute awareness of ourselves, Béjart also attempts to transform the signs of our everyday world into

---

44 John Henderson, *The First Avant-Garde*, (London: George C. Harrop, 1971), 97.

52

guideposts for our imagination. Face to face, we meet this ideal in such works as *Dichterliebe* and *Petrouchka* where symbols, both personal and private, either must draw the viewer into their midst or exclude him entirely.

As an example, when the dancer in Béjart's *Petrouchka* walks with an uncertain gait through a wall of mirrors, we, as spectators, are unaware of what he will find. Is he meant to examine his inner soul-state through seeing his reflection or to appear lost in a state of illusion? In the character of Petrouchka, Béjart creates a tragic figure, oversensitized and in search of an inner-self. Still, the use of the mirror is never really clarified. To a lesser degree, when the ballet mistress in *Gaîté Parisienne* commands her protegé to dance, classroom scenes alternate with those of France's Second Empire. In turn, the leader of soldiers, as the father figure, Napoleon III, could be said to contrast with the figure of the clown, Bim, in symbolizing eternal youth. Still we, as Béjart's audience, are never told the source of the symbols. Therefore confusion concerning the distinct relationship between choreographer and symbol may impede our appreciation of the work.

Yet another problem faced by the Symbolist poets, indicated by reviews of the period, is the futility critics felt in dealing with the illusive, dream-like substance of the drama. In such plays as *La Fille aux mains coupées* (The Girl With Severed Hands) (1893) by the poet Pierre Quillard, the structure reveals the inability of poets to reconcile the form of art with its means of presentation:

> ...a scene from the past or rather the Middle Ages. It is a silent room with a young girl who prays. A realistic *décor* would have no place in this dream drama. The dialogue in verse, spoken by the young girl, her father- a poet king with a choir of angels- is expressed in a prose which seals the action in no particular place or time.The verse portrays the soul of the characters. Is this theater? [45]

---

45 G. Roussel, "Critique d'art dramatique," *La Plume.* May 1,1894. My translation.

A majority of theatergoers of this period failed to understand the plays they saw. In introducing the viewer to the state of the dream or suggestion, the poet-playwright sought to reveal to him an alternative reality known only to his unconscious. In reality, the viewer's imagination confronted a plotless production composed of diffuse, scattered fragments in a production rarely attended by large brawling publics. The few critics who enjoyed them did not dare consider them serious art. Conversely, the seriousness of the Symbolist theater itself lay in this very subjectivity of its poet-creators. Bad reviews or not, playwrights presented their plays and would use in their productions amateur performers and unique production techniques such as spraying the stage with perfume. Anything serving the attitude of the playwright was admissible.

The dichotomy between the dramatic staging of the Symbolists and the esoteric-hermetic themes of their plays is therefore relevant to the present-day dilemma of critics *vis-à-vis* Béjart. He expresses an intensely personal attitude in works wherein the world of the unconscious serves as point of departure. Furthermore he deals with realm of spirituality or idealistic conflict such as in seminal theatrical works *Nijinsky, Clown de Dieu* and *Serafita/Serafitus*. To deal with these ideas on the stage, the dramatist needed a blend of scenic and esthetic qualities, qualities with which it is difficult to achieve a desired balance. In turn, this has caused difficulties in interpretation by critics.

To establish a relationship between Béjart's scorned productions of the seventies and the difficulty of staging serious Symbolist themes, one might consider the staging of *Madame La Mort,* by Rachilde, one of the few female dramatists who wrote for the Symbolist stage. *Madame La Mort* was criticized for its inability to stage a significant drama, illustrating that yet another problem of Symbolism lay in its being essentially a literary form:

> The first scenes of the drama unfold as somewhere in real life;
> but the second act happens entirely within the world of dream, in

the brain of a man...I tried to make believable certain hallucinations such as the struggle between Life and Death who together fight for possession of the body. [46]

In evening-length works Béjart, with filmed sequences and other devices, has made his subjective image clearer. However, an early review of one of his first staged productions, La *Reine verte* (1963), reveals how, despite the quality of performance of both of his actors (performed by Jean Babillée and Maria Césarès) and the uniqueness of stage inventions, Béjart could not make believable the struggle of Man and Death and the latter's subsequent escape into life only to be consumed by the world of the theater. A critic wrote of its Parisian première, "Béjart is a prisoner of his own conception of theater, too tempted by his own particular style." [47] For Béjart, the unfolding of style, of fusion of form, perhaps begins with the inability to say all there is to express through one medium alone.

In the ballet *Serafita/Serafitus*, produced in the mid-seventies, Béjart attempts to explain to his audiences two worlds, both of which are unreal and thus analogous to the imagined world of the ballet class. Fragments of verse from the imagined impressions of author Henry Miller, settings of the ballet class, and of Nordic *fjords* alternate in fashion analogous to sequences of dream to portray angels in heaven. Without the segments of monologue, the visually appealing and elaborately costumed danced sequences that alternate with the scenes of dancers-in-class would not be clear. Nevertheless, an alternative argument that dialogues, interspersed throughout each scene, spoil the drama's continuity is recognizable.

In like manner, the Symbolist drama sought to achieve unity of expression through the effective blending of diverse fragments of sound utterance, flowing costume, and static movement forms. Although by the early twentieth century much of the effectiveness of Symbolist *mise-en-scène* had died out, the radical experimentations

46 Henderson, *The First Avant-Garde,* 94.
47 Raphael Nataf. "La Reine verte." *Théâtre populaire.* (Paris: 1963): 3.

in combining art forms did prove advantageous and in turn produced several striking examples of successful theatrical experimentation .

Béjart's own process of experimentation commences with the decentralization of danced space to include elements of décor, sound, and cinematic framing. Therefore, if Béjart can be said to have developed a personal theory of *mise-en-scène* during the decades of the mid-twentieth century, much of it can be attributed to unconscious borrowings from principles originally employed by the Symbolists.

In our study of Béjart, these productions form the base of a new tradition through which we may interpret many of his staging principles. Béjart took inspiration from the Symbolists who used the medium of theater to evoke the undefinable spiritual quality of life and conveyed meaning through successions of images not bound to a linear plot development. Often Symbolist poets alone knew the origin of symbols they used. Final interpretation was always left to the spectator-seer. Following their example, Béjart used ballet as a means to define the multiple forces existing in dance art to implicate that art as a major social force. As creator, he alone decides the particular array of subjective symbols that he will apply to the work as a whole. He introduces these through a succession of scenes presented as collage, thus, not linear. As the production of Maeterlinck's *Pélleas et Mélisande* (1893) illustrates, the undefinable can be made theatrical, through the imagination of a particular director. Béjart's productions also rely on the subjective-expressionism of the *metteur-en-scène*.

Representing the first successful formal artistic construction for the stage, one which refused an explicit plot or theme, *Pélleas et Mélisande* created tension between the onstage narrative revealed and the spiritual meaning it symbolized. Thus, the spectator was drawn into and responded to the world of production. First performed by the *Théâtre de l'Oeuvre,* the plot of this play described the love of the widower, Goulaud, for Mélisande whom he meets while hunting. Melisande is also loved by Pélleas, who is given charge of her welfare by Genevieve, counselor of the aging Arkel. Critic Quintance Eagan describes how, in the play "Pélleas leads Mélisande to a well that is deep in the park. Fascinated by her reflection, she lets her long hair fall, then childishly playing with her wedding ring drops it into the depths."[48] The argument of the work, the subtle triangle born of suspicion, is evoked through whispered repetitive dialogue and text both elliptical and suggestive. The characters appear contained in no particular place, time, or setting.

Conceived by designer Aurelian Lugné-Poë, with décors executed by Vogler, a painter, dominant tonalities of grey and beige, sought to translate both atmosphere and essence of a philosophical stream of thought. Each form, whether evoked through subtle gesture or through décor, represented a particular symbol. The stage apparatus included no accessories or props; the scenic design itself consisted of two illusionary backdrops: heavy foliage depicting the setting where Pélleas meets Mélisande by the grotto and the grand hall of a palace. Moreover a single tableau, one wherein characters in silk, flowing costumes passed and returned from wing to wing, forming a linear design, caused the illusion of principal characters bathed in light, cast against an ensemble floating in the background. Imprecise forms coupled with predominantly grey color tones lent to the stage a mood of universality.

Maeterlinck's systematic use of repetition combined with the *décor* principle to create an overwhelming impression of awe. The characters expressed a serious demeanor suggesting innate awareness of a particular destiny. Deliberate imprecision achieved through repetitive dialogue, neutral color tones, and textures shimmered across the stage to fuse with the plot and create a mixture of innocence with fairy tale. In resisting the containment of formal intrigue or narrative, *Pélleas et Mélisande*, typical of Symbolist staging, sought to convey an attitude.

Produced on separate occasions at two Parisian theaters, Maeterlinck's *L'Intruse, Pélleas et Mélisande*, and *Les Aveugles*, all

---

48 Quintance Eaton, "Pélléas et Mélisande: Masterpiece Once and Forever", San Francisco Opera program notes: Fall, 1979.

illustrate a particular use of stage movement, lighting, and sound that together, give off an air of mystery in forming the essence of one essential symbol. The spirituality of Maeterlinck's tale of a husband, wife, and lover, was judged by critics to possess the completeness and harmony normally conveyed by an impressionist canvas. The powerful impression of the deceptively simple plot of *Pélleas et Mélisande*, based on systematic suggestion, conveys the sense of "non knowing." Conversely, the audience's heightened perception came from the anticipation that something occult and sinister was about to occur. This aura of anticipation lent an air of "sameness" to plays of the period. Sometimes an audience was asked to "pretend" that an allegory did indeed exist. In all plays, absence of action and simplicity of *décor* accounted for layers of suggested meaning.

In comparison, the dance of Loïe Fuller, first performed at the *Théâtre d'Art* of Paul Fort in 1891 survived as an example of a different point of departure of Symbolist stagings of the period, one which centered on dance. Fuller was one of the first to show that dance was archetypal, and did not need to delineate the plot of a particular story. Her dance enabled the Symbolists to reclaim the poetic property of music as the embodiment of the ideal form. As theorist Frank Kermode explained in his article, "Poet and Dancer before Diaghilev," Loïe Fuller represented to a greater degree the late nineteenth-century avant-garde than any orthodox ballerina. "In the writings of Baudelaire and in the criticism of Théophile Gauthier," Kermode explained, "the human, palpable element counts for much, but in the age of Mallarmé, the dancer is not a woman, she is dead, yet flesh and bone."[49] Fuller served as the visual expression of the poem, in Mallarmé's words, expressing through the medium of dance what words could not. She introduced to the nineteenth century the concept of "happening," a performance which defied all definition in being both radiant and homogenous:

---

49 J.F.Kermode, "Poet and Dancer before Diaghilev." *Partisan Review* (February 1961): 48, 71-2.

> Mallarmé wrote how Fuller, by the prodigious effect of short cuts and leaps with a handwriting of the body [said] what it would take entire paragraphs of prose, both in dialogue and in description to express in the written form; a poem thus freed from any apparatus of scribe. [50]

Fuller's theater used colored lights and long wooden wands. Although untrained in the classical sense, she used undulating arm movements and patterns of quick running steps to compensate for her short, stocky, stature. Her shape was ephemeral; to the poets who saw her perform, her art seemed to probe the dream vision that they had coveted for the stage for so long.

Kermode further explained how Fuller was viewed as a *majestueuse ouverture*, a reality beyond flux or vision of the infinite achieved through dance. When Diaghilev arrived, Kermode relates, and in the first *Ballets Russes* season overwhelmed the senses through a fusion of music, color, and stage design which was guided by the dancer, Fuller was remembered by audiences as having been first to do it.[51]

Because the silence of Fuller's dance articulated as much to the late nineteenth-century stage as the words of its poet-creators seeking a total work of art, spectators became aware of silence emerging as a principle of stage form or *mise-en-scène*. Thus, to compare Béjart's present-day productions to Symbolist stagings requires not only that all stage elements participate in a continuous process of ambiguity and suggestion revolving around a particular symbol, but also that the levels of signification represented onstage also denote an even deeper layer of meaning which is not readily apparent.

In the large spectacle productions of Béjart's ballets of the eighties, symbolized by nebulous forms, repetition in dialogue, and symbolic patterns of movement, echoes abound of *mises-en-scène* of the Symbolists a century before. At times, only one or two steps

---

50 Stéphane Mallarmé. "Divinations." *The First Avant-Garde*, trans: J. Henderson 33.
51 Kermode, 77.

performed in isolation in a specific direction define the dancer onstage. The movement relates to Béjart's particular scenic arrangement, of which he alone is aware. On many occasions, he is not so concerned with the way his elements are linked choreographically as whether they are readable on the particular level or "code" of the *mise-en-scène* he constructs.

Like the Symbolist poets of nearly a century before, Béjart's concern is not so much with communication as with identification through staging of a sublime presence conveyed through images composed of a fusion of performance symbols. Like the aforementioned poets and with echoes of Mallarmé's symbol of the dancer who "spoke" what words cannot, Béjart has tried to suggest the deeper layers of literary meaning through movement and physical form. Perhaps, like the Symbolists, his own innovations onstage of the mid-twentieth century do survive if only to serve as transitions for other theatrical forms.

Béjart's range of experimentation has been broadest in works not relying on a literary base, but on more obscure meanings. Static poses used as motifs, obscure hermetic symbols, and themes conveying the basic impulses of humanity: love, hate, joy, or anguish, appear repeatedly. One of Béjart's most effective stagings employing principles of Symbolism is seen in the evening-length *Pli selon phi* created in the late seventies. This work, employing multiple codes of communication, uses Mallarmé's poem as its base and illustrates Béjart's technique of relating movement to sound as a basic tenet of style. In each of the work's five musical scores, Béjart incorporates specific devices which cumulatively cause the effect of a succession of surrealist forms. In the first musical segment, *Tombeau,* followed by three segments entitled *Improvisations sur Mallarmé,* followed by *Don,* the visual imagery of *décor,* of movement, and of subtle shifting of musical tones, is guided by and interdependent of the improvised movements of the dancer. The *décor* partitions are interchangeable and can be linked or shown onstage alone. For this particular work the *décor* of the stage consists of the framed silhouette of a mosque whose towering frames, through deliberate slowness, change the parameters of suggestion.

As defined by Béjart, *Pli selon pli* is a form of "static dance." Characters appear and perform for brief, five-minute intervals and depart. They exit, they reappear, and they repeat a pattern of steps as though to reiterate a particular code or symbol. A dancer depicting the sinister Figure in Black, whose costume sweeps across the stage is faceless, wearing a featureless mask. His equally faceless partner, the Girl in Green, complements his obscurity as the denial of individual expression. She first appears out of place, wearing a ballet tunic and tights. Using only a few wooden chairs as props for an austere set, Béjart causes the figures to form an endless series of geometrical shapes which, for an instant, are poised in equilibrium, then suddenly appear off-balance. *Pli selon pli* has no plot. Its sound consists of text recitation, electronic music, and silence, which alternate throughout.

In *Tombeau*, performed to the text by Mallarmé, *Un Peu Profond Ruisseau calomnie la mort* (A shallow stream slanders death), dancers concealed in white masks contrasting with flowing black robes appear against a *décor* of three or four chairs on which stand three figures. The stillness of their pose contrasts with the flowing imagery of other dancers moving in counter directions across the stage. There are no encounters, only suggestions of meetings, which occur in silhouette as patterns that flow, jar, and then separate to achieve deliberate narrative ambiguity.

Concerning *Tombeau*, Béjart is only concerned with what the respective chance encounters of dancers *suggest* to the spectator. In the integration of form, space, and sound, no element is left unattended by the others. On one plane there is music, itself composed of fragmented sound segments composed by Pierre Boulez, whispered patterns of dialogue, and silence; on another there is form. Although designs are simple, the slightest movement of *décor*, as with the slightest shift in the physical attitude of performers, causes the stage to assume a different perspective. The dance is personal and vague, so that spectators must try to decipher the hidden, esoteric meaning of symbols that interact almost abstractly, as though nothing really has taken place.

In the midst of these shifting forms, Béjart introduces another aspect of division. A semi-nude figure wanders aimlessly, threatened by the constantly shifting black forms which oppose him in the shape of a chorus. The figure is Béjart's poet, accompanied by a girl who, in flowing robes, appears to command his movements. Although she herself does not perform, her presence introduces tension which causes in turn a subtle shift in imagery. Throughout its performance a voice whispers in varying degrees of intensity, *A la nu accablant tu* (staggering, you, nude) implying diverse meanings.

All or selected verses of five short stanzas on which the work's performance are based are recited using fragments of text. Sounds, deep and cavernous, that, although barely audible, enhance interactions between performers, also reveal hidden personal layers of meaning. On all levels of representation, whether text, movement, or stage design, moods of foreboding sustain and guide the performance. In the control and juxtaposition of elements of *mise-en-scène, Pli selon pli* expresses a myriad of interpretations through a vast array of interconnected symbols.

In *Pli selon pli*, the figure of the poet commands the indeterminancy of form on all levels. Throughout the work's five partitions his stance determines the unstable presence of the stage around which is created the defining gesture in its pureness. Secondly, in portraying the poet's companionship with the Woman in Green, Béjart uses color to emphasize opposite extremes: the tension between evil and good and between the divine and the satanic. Brevity of costume, symbolizing successive degrees of purity, also functions to unmask artifice.

In the second danced sequence, *Improvisation sur Mallarmé II*, the poet appears as his own double. As a robed statue, he stands atop a pedestal centerstage and entices his female complice to remove his robes. Through movements comprised of jerky, hip-swinging, quick tempoed steps, she crosses the stage, flirting first with the audience, then with the poet. For several minutes she serves as antithesis of the goddess. She is instead a vamp whose performance is meant to seduce. Into this sequence Béjart interjects, ironically, the figure of the goddess-vamp, causing the sequence as a whole to interrupt the serious tone of the earlier partitions and in so doing act as their complement.

Yet this comedy is controlled and meshes within the framework Béjart intends. The statue's deliberate, slow "unveiling" of robes is effective because it is performed surreptitiously. Although this score and consequent stage action appear comical, its function is of supreme importance in the total design Béjart gives to the unfolding of each performative element of his stage.

Pli selon pli thus becomes a highly organized performance of multi-theater that uses many of the devices of the Symbolists to produce esoteric or hermeneutic meanings. Performers suggest the presence of eavesdroppers, who function in relationship to the *mise-en-scène* in movement sequences that, while appearing to be improvised, are carefully controlled.

In all of Béjart's staged works of this period, there appear patterns of energetic movement that rechannel the choreographers own desire to be openly understood or "read" by the spectator. Whereas in *Dichterliebe*, the recurring image of the Hero, around which three dancers symbolizing "graces" repeatedly compose the form of a circle, suggests both mythical harmony and "knowingness," in *La Symphonie pour un homme seul,* the sensual meaning of a woman's arm, rapidly circling, carries a meaning which is non--erotic, that by its thrust and weight dynamic becomes a symbol of psychological discharge and appeasement. In both works, a single isolated pose or repeated gesture achieves closure and gives to the the process of "decoding" the work as a whole, a tacit form of reference and readability.

Thus Béjart, through the inital processes of suggestion, and of manipulation of his symbols, pre-judges his spectator's response through the use and refusal of conventional patterns of classical ballet. In using movement as but one variant of total performance, he makes us all the more aware of its power as symbol in the heritage of total theater performance. Jean-François Lyotard suggests that the aspirations of modernism could by fused in the analogous body movements and imaginary paths of the dance. In his essay "The Tensor," Leotard refers to the sacred dance understood by the philosopher, Friedrich Nietzsche:

> To understand, to be intelligent, is not our overriding passion. We strive instead to be set in motion. This is why our passion would be more like the dance that Nietzsche wanted and that Cunningham and Cage continue to look for.[52]

In *The Birth of Tragedy,* Nietzsche casts the dythyrambic dance of the satyr as the essence of dionysian frenzy. Nietzsche's introduction of the figure of the dance, revealed by impulsive, chaotic movements of the satyr as counterpart to Apollonian form, evokes the metaphor of the dance as an attribute of the being who "in bearing the heaviest destiny on his shoulders...is yet the brightest and most transcendent of spirits."[53] Introduced as a presence throughout Nietzsche's text to describe the pulsating energy of Dionysus, hence creation in the continuous process of becoming, dance is not only the principal activity of the satyr but the one through which he reconciles the principles of created form and created becoming. In the world of the demi-god, the satyr, half-man and half-goat, both destroys and creates in his frenzied dance.

It is perhaps through the aesthetic dynamic of Nietzsche that we can define the image of Béjart's dancer as one who is less dependent on form (hence on the classical aesthetic attributed to ballet) than on energy and force through which to use art as a weapon

---

52 Jean-François Lyotard, *The Lyotard Reader,* edited by Andrew Benjamin, (Cambridge: Basil Blackwell, 1989), 8-9.
53 Friedrich Nietzsche, *Thus Spake Zarathustra.* trans: Thomas Common, (New York: Gordon Press, 1974), 9.

against conflicting forces of modernity.   Beginning with art, and proceeding to religion, politics and ethics, thus to all of the domains of thought that have preoccupied the twentieth century, we can discover Nietzsche's portrayal of the will as the innermost torce of being and of power. It is through this channeling of power in the creation of "form" in the dance that Zarathustra, the philosopher, considers dance as the highest activity of man.   He cautions his followers, "None of you has learned to dance as a man ought to dance."   In the section of the work entitled *The Second Dance Song*, Nietzsche predicts that the end of the cycle will precede nightfall or death in a continuous succession of returns.   Here, Nietzsche again employs the dance metaphor as a fundamental figure of his thought.

In an early chapter of his text, *Danser Sa Vie*, Garaudy, once again, echoes the experience of Béjart in stating that life, viewed as performance, should be man's highest goal and is capable of establishing the highest rapport between ourselves and the forces referred to by Nietzsche as belonging to primordial nature. As a system of signs onto which we project our lives, dance becomes a metaphor that pulsates with what Nietzsche has called "the greatest potential energy," its continuous relationship with the processes of becoming. In the preface to the same text, Béjart has written of *The Birth of Tragedy*:

> Alors, comme disait Nietzsche
> l' esclave est libre, alors se brisent
> toutes les barrières rigides et hostiles
> que la misère, l'arbitraire, la mode
> insolente ont établies entre les hommes.
> Maintenant, par l'évangile de l'harmonie
> universelle, chacun se sent avec son
> prochain, non seulement réuni,
> réconcilié, fondu, mais encore identique
> en soi, comme si s'était déchiré le voile
> de Maia. [54]

---

54 Garaudy, *Danser Sa Vie*, 92.

As Nietzsche declared, the slave is free;
then all barriers, rigid and hostile, are broken,
that misery, arbitrariness, and insolent fashion
have established among men.
Now, by the truth of universal harmony,
each feels at one with his neighbor, not only reunited,
reconciled, founded, but identical in
Selfhood. As if the Maian veil were torn.

Through his view of the dancer-figure both as figure of language and as metaphor signifying the reinterpretation of the present, Béjart brings into play the Nietzschian dynamic of destruction and of creation. He employs these as creative system, not only in his choice of the dancer-protagonist through which he evokes a metaphor, but also through his conception of spectacle itself.

Béjart's protagonist is the dancer whose gesture on stage, freed from the constraint of classicism, commands both form (of Apollo) and force (of Dionysus) enacting the tragic figure. It is the dancer who forms the center of Béjart's *mise-en-scène*; it is the dancer whose static poses and leaps, whose use of non-conventional gestures and force, fuse within the parameters of classical ballet technique (which Béjart never totally abandons) to create on the stage a new interweaving of movement that is both Apollonian and Dionysian in its ability to evoke the sublime and to shock.

However, it is also through the will to "destroy" a masterpiece, as Béjart's earlier ballets exhibit, that the Dionysian aspect of Béjart's representation onstage emerges. Whereas form integrates established principles of décor into scenic action, onstage action into dialogue, and lighting designs into the process of performance, it also destroys the literary structure of the work and rearranges it, causing the occurrence of *métissage*. This Dionysian destruction of form brings the spectator face to face with images which on one level may displease, yet on another, provide consideration of their value. Destruction gives necessary new life to the classic image. It is a ritual necessary to creation, a function that is vital in allowing the spectator to transcend the external framework of a work of art.

In *Notre Faust*, inspired by Goethe, in *Le Molière imaginaire*, based on characterizations of the seventeenth century French playwright, and in *Romeo et Juliette*, based on Shakespeare, Béjart has established particular principles effecting onstage form to literary content. Through this lens, the spectator must decipher the relationship between onstage manifestations of *métissage* and the original work on which they are based as well as their particular relationship to the realm of political or social *hors-texte* to which they refer. In *Notre Faust*, a juxtaposition of sound occurs on one level between a Bach Mass and an Argentinian tango, while on another costumes conceived in richly colored brocades starkly contrast with the neutral tones of *décor*. Both juxtapositions symbolically suggest opposing realms of sacred and profane. Thus, witnessing violation of form and experiencing tension occurring between the elements of destruction, on one hand, and the original form of the literary work on the other, the spectator is prodded to a heightened awareness from the spectacle. It is this effect on the spectator that gives the theater its vitality. Through this act of destroying, the dancer brings a new form into play through his enigmatic presence.

In a larger sense, dispersion and disassembling of sections of spoken text within works staged by Béjart allow him to replicate the fundamental energies of the artist described by Nietszche. In Béjart's destruction of text, the dancer's body emerges and is used as a conveyor of energy through which the spectator discovers that he may act as judge and anticipate, through the medium of the stage, communion with his unconscious.

In allowing the spectator this choice, Béjart's stage becomes the scene of a double representation, that of the hybrid form he chooses to present and that of the tacit remembering by the spectator of its literary base. We can now add to these latter systems of theatrical representation a third, espoused by Antonin Artaud in *Le Théâtre et son double*. Artaud privileges unspoken sound over speech and sees gesture as a return to a fundamental level of sensory experience, which creates onstage, through the continual unfolding of hieroglyph, a poetry. In itself, this expression constitutes a fundamental realm of knowing. It is, furthermore, this principle of fusion of signs in the wake of initial destruction of "verbal text" that is of importance in implementing a staging consisting of multiple codes or signatures. On this stage, all accessible means are used to evoke a language that is non-representational through the principle of *mise-en-scène*. Through this manifestation, destruction of the authorly text occurs almost surreptitiously, causing, through the imprint on the senses, the principle of cruelty to emerge as a gesture of force and assertion. Artaud thus describes the *mise-en-scène* of the Balinese dance:

> En somme les Balinais réalisent, avec la plus extrême rigueur, l'idée du théâtre pur, où tout, conception comme réalisation, ne vaut d'existence que par son degré d'objectivation sur la scène. Ils démontrent victorieusement la prépondérence absolue du metteur-en-scène dont le pouvoir de création élimine des mots. Les thèmes sont vagues, abstraits, extrêmement généraux. Seul, leur donne vie, le foisonnement compliqué de tous les artifices scéniques qui imposent à notre esprit comme l'idée d'une métaphysique tirée d'une utilisation nouvelle du geste et de la voix. [55]

> In summary, the Balinese realize, with the most extreme rigor the idea of pure theater, where all, conception as realization, is worth, only exists to the degree of its objectivisation on stage. Victoriously they show the absolute importance of the stage director whose powers of creation eliminate words. Subjects are vague, abstract, extremely open. Only the complex abundance of scenic artifice that is imposed on our spirit as the idea of a metaphysics gleaned from a new use of the gesture and of the voice, gives them life.

---

55 Artaud, *Le Théâtre et son double.* 82.

68

The emphasis that Artaud places on the elimination of word in precising a panegyric of verbal text, in favor of a new form derived from a "metaphysics"of gesture and voice causes us to consider the primary role Béjart accords to the mixture of movement and voice as a performative device. We may also return to the idea of Mallarmé, where the dance, embodying multiple modes of communication, is able to suggest more readily than words and to activate meaning through a metaphor that is primarily spatial. Artaud continues:

> Ces signes spirituels ont un sens précis, qui ne nous frappe plus qu'intuitivement, mais avec assez de violence pour rendre inutile toute traduction dans un langage logique et discursif. [56]

> These spiritual signs have a precise sense, that strikes us more than intuitively, but with enough violence so as to render useless all translation into a logical and discursive language.

Movement and, in particular, gesture, in Artaud's system and in Béjart's, embody a particular re-channeling of dynamic forces that function in a complex interweaving of roots linking the theater, in essence, to a complex play of realities.

Finally, Artaud cites *le jeu eminemment realiste du double qui s'éffare des apparitions de l'au-délà* (the eminently realistic game of the double that frightens with spectres of the beyond). As though through the presence of the theater itself, a transcendent, more essential realm were possible.

I believe that Béjart has created a similar energetic for his stage both in his concern for setting up different relations of tension among its elements, and in his fusing of vocal sound with movement patterns that evolve from enactment of a specific gesture repeated throughout a work's performance. Such is the gesture in Béjart's spectacle work, *Le Molière imaginaire,* used to indicate rupture, a mid-performance transformation or metamorphosis in which the

---

56 Ibid.

historical world is linked to that of the stage and of the senses. This transformation is often represented by the performance of a minimal gesture in profile. Such minimal gestures as arching the back or flexing the foot have formal meaning and function as notable codes or signatures. Performed on a stage where ornate *décors* are often framed by a wooden barre, the gestures symbolize social attitudes. The barre itself represents the constraints and irony of the everyday world and is intended to posit the spectator's gaze.

Through the writings of Artaud, we are led to analyze the role Béjart gives to destruction as a reordering of aesthetic form in order to create a prospective art. We are also led to discover, in accordance with Nietzsche's Dionysian/Apollonian construct, an aspect of sacredness in Béjart's dance that imagines performance as embodying a transcendental force. Each aesthetic presents a process of freeing and separation by which his art emerges as a triumphal, purer entity.

Béjart's dance spectacle refuses to focus on gender roles normally ascribed to ballet, thus engendering debate on its role as modernist expression. In this debate, Artaud's thoughts may again be helpful. Artaud outlines certain processes wherein writing, through a system of gesture or kinesthetics, is posited as a process of theatrical form. Also instructive to understanding this system as presented by Artaud and, by analogy, in Béjart's spectacle works of the seventies and eighties, is Jacques Derrida's essay, *La Clôture de la représentation*. For Derrida, the text when activated by *jeu* or play becomes, in itself, theatrical. Derrida's reading would seem to include the idea of text on Artaud's stage both in terms of language and within the context of what Artaud defines as *cruauté*. The idea of the interchangeability of writing (in which occurs an infinite interplay of substitutions) is useful in the analysis of Artaud and of Béjart. In both systems of representation, the relationship of these element is indeterminate, as is their interrelationship with a social political *hors texte* (or reality beyond the representation). This series of relationships becomes extremely important in the analysis not only of the concept of *cruauté*, but also of Béjart's belief that ballets should contain a social message. In these works, the skillful use of symbols to convey extreme sensual opposites or attitudes is frequently cast in a context wherein dance, taken as *écriture,* opposes its value as traditional art. The result is the creation of oppositions between ballet movement vocabularies and modern dance forms, between the gesture as symbol and as functioning within the corpus of a coded technique.

In his essay, Jacques Derrida alludes to Artaud's statement, that *La Danse, et par conséquent le théâtre n'ont pas encore commencé à exister* (Dance, and consequently theater have not yet begun to exist).[57] Throughout his essay he speaks of Artaud's view of theater as an act of life, an act of affirmation, which "to be born," must first die as it currently exists. Artaud defines *cruauté* as necessity and the theater of cruelty as being therefore an affirmation of life itself, which is continual. Destruction, in Artaud's thought, is a necessary *"rite de passage"* through which the theater can be reborn or re-emerge. *De même le théâtre est un mal parce qu'il est l'équilibre supreme qui ne s'acquiert pas sans destruction* (Besides the theater is an evil because it represents the supreme equilibrium which is not acquired without destruction).[58]

If, in following the thought of Artaud, destruction is part of a necessary act through which theater is reborn, with the faintest trace of its past reeducating it's organs toward a new or purer rebirth, it is also ahistoric. It is impossible for life, in echoing an infinite series of traces, through the processes of representation, to occur more than once. We may also apply Derrida's statement to Béjart's redirection of literary elements in the creation of a hybrid form based on literary metaphor.

Thus, the ideal of theater, as conceived by Artaud, like that of dance, envisioned by Béjart, becomes a force wherein every element represents an embryonic unfolding. In the unfolding process it reveals the obvious impossibility of a limited stage or one controlled

---

57 Derrida. *L'Ecriture et la différence* (Paris: Seuil, 1972), 341.
58 Artaud, *Le Théâtre et son double*, 46.

by a specific text. Similarly, *mise-en-scène* becomes not only accessory to text, but also a *sur-text* or evocation through means which are at once primordial and present. Through the fusion of gesture and intonated sound, and with every other means of representation at Béjart's disposal, a system of signs emerges that, in Artaud's theory, cannot be considered apart from presence.

In Derrida's essay, writing, like virtual theater, is really an infinite substitution of text connoting, within each representation, multiple codes of meaning. Thus, Béjart's dance, like Artaud's stage, can be termed an outgrowth of an eternal system of traces which form a primordial writing. The concept of *cruauté*, like life itself, is contained in a theater perpetually and continuously present, whose "actuality" and purpose are not dissimilar to those of Béjart's stated creation of "the same ballet":

> L'art théâtral doit être le lieu primordial et privilegié de cette destruction de l'imitation: plus qu'un autre il a été marqué par ce travail de représentation totale dans laquelle l'affirmation de la vie se laisse dédoubler et creuser par la négation. Cette représentation, dont la structure s'imprime non seulement dans l'art mais dans toute la culture occidentale (ses religions, ses philosophies, sa politique), désigne donc plus qu'un type particulier de construction théâtrale C'est pourquoi la question qui se pose à nous aujourd'hui excède largement la téchnologie théâtrale. 59

> Theatrical art must be the primordial and privileged space of this destruction of imitation. More than anything else it has been marked by this effort at total representation in which the affirmation of life is allowed to be expanded and hollowed out by negation. This representation, whose structure is imprinted not only in art but also in all Western culture (its religions, its philosophies, and its politics) designates then more than a particular type of theatrical construction. That is why the question asked of us today greatly surpasses theatrical technology.

---

59 Derrida, *L'Ecriture et la différence*, 344.

In his study of Artaud's theatrical system, Jacques Derrida cites the playwright's use of the non-literal and non-representational aspects of theater that are sensed, thus allowing the audience to experience a heightened degree of awareness through the mixing of non-traditional modes of sound, lighting, and *décor*. Yet Derrida also emphasized the totality of the realm this theater represents. In this theater, where unuttered speech is advocated over spoken text, where the *geste* is capable of illustrating essential threatening ideas, a representation repeated infinitely both activates a *tableau* and illustrates a poetry that is at once visual and auditory:

> ....très difficile et complexe revêt de multiples aspects: elle revêt d'abord ceux de tous les moyens d'expression utilisables sur une scène comme musique, danse, plastique, pantomime, mimique, gesticulation, intonations, architecture, éclairage et décor.[60]

> ...very difficult and complex seen from multiple points of view: it at first addresses all of usable means of expression on the stage such as music, dance, pantomime, plastic, mime, gesture, intonation, architecture, lighting, and décor.

This dynamic of senses, extended to include Béjart's own gradual unfolding of onstage space, is rendered on several planes simultaneously. Using symbols to stand for ideas, Béjart blends events from autobiography with those of fantasy, creating a "vertical" axis. This axis invokes a character portrayal that is both confident and ambiguous. In like manner, using interrelations of color, sound, form, and movement to represent various correspondences of senses, Béjart presents an allegory that operates horizontally to provide, during performance, a separate cognitive foundation. In each system, elements of dream and suggestion serve as a system of knowledge and identification. Equally important, and threaded throughout both theories, is the idea of the hieroglyph embodying a simultaneous coming together of many forms.

---

60 Artaud, *Le Théâtre et son double*, 57-8.

73

In his essay, *Le Théâtre de la cruauté chasse Dieu de la scène* (The theater of cruelty chases God from the stage), Artaud vehemently affirms a god as author who has control of the text. In denying this god its power, Artaud calls forth a presence akin to Nietzsche's "super man." In denying this god, his theater affirms its selfhood and transforms the act of representation into a presence of "primary" performance. This assertion of presentness defies the limits of performance, yet gives to what occurs on a stage its own unique freedom and sense of the universal. In turn, this freedom gives way to representation which, in issuing from the *espace clos du dedans de soi* (the closed space from within the self),[61] also reaffirms the concept of *représentation originaire* by asserting the representation and implying its twin vision of its selfhood.

Through Derrida's interpretation of the aesthetic frame, which both transcends and is contained within the limits of spectacle, determining the limits or boundaries of the act of performance becomes problematic. The integrity of performance required by Artaud demands that the theater belong, through its energy and form, to a performance aesthetic capable of transcending itself. He also assures us that dance, in following the primitive ritual of the Balinese, assumes the role of a superior force armed with ritual gestures destined to form indelible impressions on our senses.

Artaud explains the spell of sacredness that dance can produce and the significance of its assertive and deliberate act in the choreography of Béjart in ballets such as *L'Oiseau de feu* and in his stagings as *Cinq Nō modernes*. Artaud insists upon its capacity to fuse with a given political or social reality beyond the parameters of the stage. Key to understanding Béjart's wish to "free" dance from what he has referred to as the *mépris du corps* (disdain of the flesh) of classicism is Derrida's idea of immediacy as it applies to representation. This element of presentness ascribes to the theater a

---

61 Derrida, *L'Ecriture et la différence*, 349.

necessity and an authority capable, through the act of representation, of recalling onstage a presence that is primordial.

> La représentation cruelle doit m'investir. Et la non-représentation est donc représentation originaire, si représentation signifie aussi déploiement d'un volume, d'un milieu à plusieurs dimensions, expérience productrice de son propre espace. Espacement, c'est à dire production d'un espace qu'aucune parole ne saurait résumer ou comprendre. [62]

> Cruel representation must empower me. And non-representation is then original being, if representation also signifies deployment of a volume, of a milieu with several dimensions, a productive experience of one's personal space. Spacing, that is to say, production of a space that no word can summarize nor understand.

For Artaud, the premordiality of energy and form revolved around a particular conception and application of language and gesture that fuses within a stage and whose power resides in its *mise-en-scène*. If one considers Artaud's conception of theatrical language as *mise-en-scène,* one can perceive in Béjart a similar framework wherein movement, in being the dominant manifestation of language, attains the sacred.

Artaud describes language as being all that is manifested and expressed on the stage, a poetry containing, among others, the expressions of music, dance, mimicry, gesture, and décor. Language, in being separate from text, permits the theater to differentiate itself from mere *parole* (speech). This differentiation, Artaud asserts, places speech apart from the stage, causing it to belong, instead, to literature. Artaud distinguishes between words and the stage of *idées au vol* (ideas in flight) that are visible as a kind of supreme presentness involved in what he has designated as *représentation originaire*:

---

62 Ibid., 348.

Il est juste que le théâtre demeure le lieu de passage le plus
éfficace et le plus actif de ces immenses ébranlements
analogiques où l'on arrête les idées au vol. [63]

It is reasonable that theater remain the most efficient and most
active site of the passing of these immense analogous shocks
wherein ideas are arrested in flight.

For Artaud, as for Béjart, these *idées au vol* are expressed in sound by
means of incantations formed through the modulations of the throat,
through noises, and inaudible whisperings of dreams, where the need
for audible word is eliminated. Doing away with the concept of *Dieu
auteur*, and the logocentric text wherein words are the supreme
power, occurs when the concept of language is expanded to include
sound as but one of many dimensions.

In the essay, *Théâtre oriental et théâtre occidental*, Artaud
explains that this language necessarily frames itself in the idea of
mise-en-scène and that, in so doing, the latter is capable of reaching
beyond the text in an attempt to grasp the mystical presence of the
beyond. The *mise-en-scène* must be *comme la matérialisation visuelle
et plastique de la parole* (As the plastic and visual materialization of
word).[64] For Artaud, words allude only to psychological realities
whereas the true domain of the theater lies elsewhere, in its
possibilites *d'expression dynamique et dans l' espace opposées aux
possibilités de l' expression par la parole dialoguée* (of dynamic
expression in space opposed to to possibilities of dialogical
expression).[65]

The staging of Béjart's spectacle works of the seventies and
eighties may be said to express the dynamic of language envisioned
by Artaud in function of its resolving and establishing a microcosm
embodying multiple systems of meaning. Motifs are repeated through

---

63 Artaud, *Le Théâtre et son double*, 169.
64 Ibid., 106.
65 Ibid., 139.

such codings as color, movement patterns, lighting, and the placement of devices and props onstage to effect a particular point of view. In his stagings, Béjart has used this idea of language to invoke themes of emotional preoccupations of conscience in contemporary life. Echoing Artaud's desire that the theater engage itself, that its duty is to concern itself both with the anguish and with the longing of the future, Béjart's choreography of the mid-twentieth century incarnates a spectacle that is vital in directly addressing, decade by decade, the questions of our present.

Hybridness and fragmentation enrich a larger conception of form on the stage, that of totality and of the dominance of its *mise-en-scène*. Thus, Artaud's *idées au vol* define for language an aggressive physical assertion in constantly recalling the gesture of the Balinese ritual. For Artaud, the Balinese with their dance consisting of angular forms, of starkly delineated attitudes, of subtle curves define a physical language that can extend beyond the parameters of Western dance, and this gives to the art of gesture a transcendental power. Artaud, as well, places importance on the physicality of the gesture as principal agent of destruction.

In Béjart's aesthetic, the explicit gesture becomes the tacit link through which spectators decipher readability. In succumbing to the power of the hieroglyph on stage, the spectator must, in turn, sense himself within the boundary of an aesthetic space that cannot be contained and that exceeds the boundary of representation through the diversity of its elements.

Artaud, in considering the Balinese ritual, explains the device of the gesture that through its surety and deliberateness posits onstage a spiritual state. According to Artaud, the theater should be able to invoke the state of the trance or spell and in so doing provoke an attitude on the spectator's part. Thus, isolated physical postures, such as the glance of The Man in Béjart's seminal work, *La Symphonie pour un homme seul,* or the flexed arch in profile of the clown in *Le Molière imaginaire,* are equally important as symbols through which the gesture expands beyond the frame of the spectacle of which it is part. Through stunning effects of microphone incantation, through onstage relationships of scenic space to sound, and through the relationship of human form to lighting. Béjart creates a dance that reaches beyond to exceed our imagination.

Finally, Artaud affirms in his essay *Lettres sur le langage* the principal role attributed to gesture as virtual theater:

> De ce nouveau langage la grammaire est encore à trouver. Le geste en est la matière et la tête; et si l'on veut l'alpha et l'oméga. Il part de la NECESSITE de la parole beaucoup plus que de la parole déjà formée. [66]

> The grammar of this new language is yet to be discovered. The gesture is its matter and its head; and if one wants the alpha and omega, it derives from the necessity for speech rather than from speech already formed.

For Béjart, the sacred dance is part of a system of signs, of language extending beyond itself and involving itself, at times almost unaided by the our presence as spectators who silently witness within its ritual the concerns of our present. Moreover, it is an art of engagement in social forces, of actualizing the present. Its ancestry derives from the influence of three aesthetic systems, wherein is produced a universal system of language. In these systems of total theater, through the intangible presence of *mise-en-scène,* a new system of signs prompts the spectator to envision what may lie beyond the frame of representation.

Béjart seems to affirm that it is the theater's duty to undertake an inventory of the present, as well as the spectator's duty to respond. This is the task proposed by Béjart in echoing the fusion of the Dionysian with the Apollonian proposed by Nietzsche, the aesthetic embodiment of the *au délà* of the Symbolists, and the enactment of the sacred dance envisioned by Artaud.

---

66 Ibid., 171.

CHAPTER THREE
BEJART AND THE DANCE SPECTRUM

The purpose of this chapter is to introduce to the reader formalistic elements contained within seminal choreographies of Maurice Béjart and to organize these into representative categories centered around the use of the body and its expressive potential. During the chronological period in which the *Ballet du XXième Siècle* had its beginnings, in Europe in the mid-twentieth century, no two works conceived by Béjart drew upon the same choreographic schema. His works, however, are displayed categorically around themes displaying specific formal elements. The relationship of performance time to scenic elements, as well as the relationship of movement to sound, and to shifts in scenic space presented onstage to create mood are explored within this chapter.

An extended analysis of Béjart's choreographic style reveals, within the distinctive formal elements that emerge, an allegiance to the subjective, to the autobiographical:

> Depuis mes débuts de chorégraphe, je fais perpétuellement le même ballet, tout en tenant un journal de mes rencontres, de mes amitiés, de mes amours, de ma découverte de l'univers, soit extérieure, soit intérieure.
>
> C'est pourquoi je crois qu'il est très difficile de juger un de mes ballets sans les connaître tous, sans même connaître ceux qui sont complètement, ratés, totalement inutiles, mais précisement parce qu'ils sont utiles à une autre construction! [67]

> Since my beginnings as choreographer, I continually create the same ballet, all the while keeping a journal of my encounters, friendships, loves, the discovery of the universe whether exterior or interior.
>
> That is why I believe it is difficult to judge one of my works without knowing all of them, even those which are

---

[67] Antoine Livio, *Béjart,* 68.

completely useless or spoiled, precisely because they are useful
for another construction!

Examining the scope of Béjart's choreography reveals an amazing
diversity of form. As he has continued to use creative staging to
experiment with form, a spectrum emerges that includes, among its
many subdivisions, ballets that emerge from forms which are
symphonic, others that derive from a literary base, those that are
experimental, biological, and even mystical in scope. His
choreography may be viewed as *auteuristic*, for symbols interspersed
among these formal categories are personal and merit consideration.

Béjart never pronounces a work as complete; it is merely one
more progression along the path of a continuous evolution of form.
On this spectrum, a kaleidoscopic invention is present that never
completes itself and yet constitutes one of the more fascinating
aspects of his art. Each dance is based upon a series of movements
emanating from a seminal series of gestures. Laying his groundwork,
Béjart creates, using dance as his most important means of
representation, all the while surrounding his movements with other
levels of readability, a panoply of suggestion comprised of sound,
décor, and scenic devices. This chapter will delineate the formal
elements of this "sensual shock" and how it is used make vivid works
during a given period.

Examples of works that might be termed "biological," in their
use of formalistic elements include: *Le Sacré du printemps* (1959),
and *L'Oiseau de feu* (1971, 1992), both of which illustrate the
converging of circular form toward a specific center. Choreographed
eleven years apart, both ballets use a circular form as the principal
movement formation to convey meaning as an initiation into a totality
of choreographic design. In *Le Sacré du printemps,* the biological
mating of the chosen couple corresponds in form to the motif of a
Phoenix that rises from the center of two converging circles, each
symbolizing revolutionary cells of partisans banding together. In *Le
Sacré du printemps*, linearly developed movement stemming from a
primary circular motif is in turn juxtaposed with linearly developed

sound. Yet the basic design of the ballet could be described as one wherein two opposing circular groups converge. In merging, alternating movement patterns of dancers clothed in atmospheric costumes of partisans taunt the chosen couple. Form is revealed through danced segments of *à terre* steps which are rhythmically countercurrent to that of the chosen couple. As the biological center or nucleus, the mated couple emerges from its mass at the end of the ballet, having become whole or complete through the representation of one singular, ideal movement form. The circular or biological model of danced movement can thus also be said to symbolize the merging of individualities into union.

The ballet *L'Oiseau de feu* represents a parallel construction as representation, dependent upon the circular formation. Using choreographic motifs formulated with simple steps that are repeated directly and intently, the first motif symbolizes a group of partisan youth in quest of a leader. Critic George Jackson describes this as being "accurate as a sociologist's movement analysis of a revolutionary cell."[68] The formation given the followers of the Firebird is indeed both circular and cellular. The joining of the two circles is starkly evident when the Firebird and his followers merge with the partisans. *L'Oiseau de feu* maintains its circularity throughout, developing choreographic patterns that are spatially innovative. Continuing step patterns are "passed on" from one group to another or are performed in counterpoint. When followers of the Firebird, dressed in orange tunics, merge with the companions of the partisans, dressed in bright blue, the energy dynamic increases and is maintained until the end of the ballet. At this point, as the Firebird expires, the Phoenix actually and in formation emerges from a focused center of two circles to symbolize the birth of yet another embryonic cycle.

Another form of development used by Béjart in nascent choreographies of the *Ballet du XXième Siècle* is the operatic. In

---

68 George Jackson. "The Sensual Moment: A Letter to Friends and Colleagues on Maurice Béjart," 1972. Dance Collection, Lincoln Center Library for Performing Arts.

early staged works such as *Mathilde ou l'amour fou* (1965) or in *Les Quatre Fils Aymon* (1967) a continuous recitative woven from music, dramatic action, and set design is wielded together by numerous allegorical scenes converging around a central hero. In this form, Béjart's spectacle evidences the beginnings of what will later become his principle of *métissage*, a hybrid mixture of many elements to emerge as what is viable and new.

As a formal element, *métissage* was first explored by Béjart in *Nijinsky, Clown de Dieu*, choreographed in 1971. In choosing as his theme a ten-year period in the life of dancer, Vaslav Nijinsky, Béjart created an imagined scenario using a variety of sensory modalities. Thus, sound segments of Nijinsky's diary were alternated among classical and electronic music scores, controlled stage space, and precise, gestural movements. Composed allegorically around the actions of a central hero, portrayed as Nijinsky the dancer, formal techniques emphasized movements of the "happening" or circus overshadowing those of traditional ballet technique. Achieving on a circular stage an aura of total spectacle, a fusion of elements of costume, musical collage, verbal text, and movement revolve around a dominant theme, expressing the duality of the character of man and his double, the clown. Nijinsky, performed by Jorge Donn, perched as a wild animal upon the shoulders of a Doppelganger, portrayed by dancer Pero Dobrievitch, shouts to the audience, "Master of his art, I am a clown to make myself understood!"

In *Nijinsky, Clown de Dieu* Béjart undertook to achieve, through the use of the mask, a representation of the other or double. The clown persona enshrined the double persona of Nijinsky through the use of the text of his diary: "I will introduce myself as a clown...to make myself better understood."[69] Béjart's professed intent in his portrait ballets is to awaken his audience, to arouse them to ask questions and to articulate a dialogue with the code of music, text, and dance elements. In *Nijinsky,* each character is represented twice,

---

69 Vaslav Nijinsky. *Diary of Vaslav Nijinsky* ed. Romola Nijinsky (New York: Simon & Schuster, 1936).

both as character and as a double who is performed and conceived in both literary and theatrical senses. Nijinsky's clown, whom he perceives as his double self, emerges as superior to the figure of the dancer, because he appears as a spiritual being, at one with God. Conversely, Diaghilev's double is conceived by Béjart as a magnificent doppelganger, formed of wax and papier-maché, who marches on stilts and is thus conceived as character without real substance. Both through movement and through costume design, the ballet achieves through the presence of character and double, an instability of implied relationships and of representation itself.

Béjart's music for this ballet is a juxtaposition of nineteenth century Tchaikovsky symphonic style alternating with modern electronic partitions composed by Pierre Henry. Béjart conceives the musical signature of *Nijinsky* upon a concurrent exploration of musical frontiers to coincide with that of movement, forming a collage effect, one arranged dialectically and pitting the classical against the modern. In the second half of the ballet, entitled *Nijinsky de Dieu,* a controlled relation of sound to staging and sound to vivid sequences of red and ochre lighting, makes real the scenes of the dancer-character's subsequent loneliness and descent into madness.

Bejart also experimented with the collage form in the spectacle work, *I Trionfi di Petrarca* (1974) where he collaborated with composer Luciano Berio. The ballet became a total creation deriving from numerous encounters, exchanges of letters, sketches, and musical segments. "Certain fragments and important words of the text are perceptible within the partitions," Béjart explained, "but the argument is presented visually. The sounds on the tape montage form a polyphony of sonorous Italian language without revealing a specific text; they represent a popular, folk quality which is part of Berio's music."[70]

One of the first spectacle works to utilize a theory of combined performance of voice and dance linking resonating sound

---

70 Martine Cadieu. "Béjart et la musique," *La Nouvelle Critique* (Paris: July, 1974), 19.

with specific movements of the body, *I Trionfi di Petrarca* uses improvisation as element of performance through its use of the *danseur-chanteur* (dancer-singer). Béjart states of these *danseur-chanteurs*:

> They are not great singers, but when they know a piece of music they can sing it as well as dance it. In this manner, they can perform and sing such works as the *Cantates* of Bach. The physical force of an actor must, at times, be utilized for moments of singing; likewise, when certain jumps demand extraordinary force, the voice must be quiet. The idea is to fuse the voice and dance together without interrupting the continuity of either.[71]

In the prelude to the opening tableau, entitled *Il Trionfo dell'Amore* (the triumph of love) no orchestrated sound is used. Six dancer *mudrists*[72] appear who represent "spirits of nature" and begin to perform a combination of awkward, loosely-connected steps in a diagonal pattern across the stage. They half sing, half grunt, in coarse indistinguishable tones. As they enter the center-stage area, their sound intensifies in speed, volume, and variance of pitch until it becomes a shout. The silence which follows further enhances mood revealed through multiple dynamics of sound and movement. Sung partitions follow, evoking a different level of reality to frame the main stage action as dancer Jorge Donn, portraying the hero-poet, dances a *pas de deux* with Laure, performed by ballerina Suzanne Farrell.

The *danseur-chanteur*'s use as device is Béjart's unique creation, one he will include in later works. Combined with brown and ocre lighting, this device is fundamental to understanding Béjart's theatrical stream of effects which both enhance and surround the formal structure of the ballet, *I Trionfi di Petrarca*.

---

71 Personal Interview: Maurice Béjart, 1978.
72 Students of Mudra, the school created by Béjart in Brussels, apply to performance the combined principle of gesture, sound, and mime to create a concept deemed as that of the "total performer."

The argument of the ballet is formed by six tableaux which are based on six triumphs (or dreams) of the poet, Petrarch. All are realized with splendid special effects and props. Each principal dancer is also given a *leitmotif*, a pose through which to symbolize a particular character, thus affording a means of compartmentalizing this evening-length work into six separate scenes.

In the triumph wherein the figure of love conquers that of chastity, a chariot appears onstage bearing Laure, personified by Farrell. The scene portrays Laure as the unattainable love of Petrarch, thereby symbolizing love's suffering. Béjart's choreography in this segment centers upon the single gesture as principal delineator of character, that is repeated in the manner of a leitmotif. In this danced segment, the gesture of love becomes that of two arms outstretched, and portraying its triumph through the companion figure of the unicorn, animal of love. Embodying the triumph of love, the unicorn as symbol becomes all important as a theme expressed by diminutive movements, exemplified in the performance of dancer Rita Poelvoorde.

For the following triumph, *Il Trionfo della Guerra* (the triumph of war), expressive mimed sequences performed by Daniel Lommel as warrior use the archery contest to symbolize the poetic triumph of Mars, god of war over that of Love and its animal the unicorn.

Allegorically, the staging of this danced segment conveys that war, unless won with weapons of virtue and wisdom, will assuredly bring defeat. Only Death, revealed as the succeeding triumph, *Il Trionfo della Morte*, prevails. The symbolism of a decisive gesture of downwardly clasped hands is repeatedly invoked. In the wake of his meeting with Death with its animal, the Gorgon, the dancer-poet, performed by Jorge Donn, meets Fame and its companion, the Phoenix. Constituting the fifth triumph, fame is, in turn, challenged by the triumphs of time and of eternity, wherein names are erased, monuments crumble, and glory is forgotten. In the sixth partition of the ballet, entitled *Il Trionfo del Tempo* (the triumph of time), Béjart has dancer Nikolas Ek move across the stage on stilts, gazing upon a blue veil that covers the entirety of scenic space under which dancers are positioned to rise and fall, so as to resemble tossing waves. Ek portrays the figure of Time, in consortium with dancer Ivan Marko who performs with Ek as the shadow, or double image. Together, their performance as *pas de deux*, symbolizes the slow passage of Time toward Eternity, signifying the seventh triumph of the poet. Concurrent with the deliberate sound of the steathily marching steps, evoked metaphorically as sounds of a metronome, time's duality and slow passage toward eternity unfolds as narrative by means of an exposition of elaborate props and partitions. Each carefully isolated *pas de deux* depicts a single Petrarchian triumph. The ballet was first performed against opulent frescoes painted with designs of Botticelli on the stage of the Boboli Gardens of Florence, Italy. It was later presented in New York at the Brooklyn Academy of Music in 1969.

The ballet illustrates, perhaps better than any other, the principle of multi-art developed by Béjart at Mudra, his school in Brussels. The lighting design, through which is cast onstage an image of fallen dead leaves, gives to the work a mood of remoteness. In the richness of its baroque design, *I Trionfi di Petrarca* foreshadows Béjart's use of the ornate operatic form

In direct contrast to the literary form, developed around the theme of one singular character, the operatic form uses distinct and self-sufficient symbols and fragments of action that are dominated by subjective meanings accessible only to their creator. In this form, separate yet interdependent performed segments of sound, movement, and scenic space dominate the stage. In such ballets as *Baudelaire* (1965), *Bhakti* (1969), *Serafita/Serafitus* (1974), and *Ce que l'amour me dit* (1978), elements of this form are visible. Multitheater, a spectacle wherein dance is seen as but one formal element of a collage, provides yet another primary context through which a code of symbols represents the literary form.

Béjart's literary works are numerous and frequently rely on the device of suggestion. In *Baudelaire* (1967), bright glaring colors contrast with purer lines of classical technique and serve to enhance the more fundamental movements of modern dance. Irreconcilable opposites presented in its choreography, in turn, echo in lyrics the modernist vision of the artist who is both hero and outcast of the city.

For his text to *Baudelaire*, Béjart chose portions of verse from the poems, *Jet d'eau, L'Etranger, and Fusées*, taken from Baudelaire's collection of poems, *Les Fleurs du mal.* For the musical score, Pierre Henry enjoined composed partitions of *musique concrète* to impressionist chords of Debussy. These were, in turn, sung by dancers in the manner of an operatic recitative. When dancer Angele Albrecht stood before a microphone to "sing" the score to Tchaikovsky's *Swan Lake,* the musical became ironic as the dancer-turned-singer-interlocutress sustained as shock the transference among different modes of performance. This sensation of shock, which began as an aural assault on the senses, transferred to the visual realm, repressing any sense of otherness or of contradiction. For the ballet's concluding sequence, five couples, performing in tandem, created on a circular stage images of Baudelaire's poem: *Jet d'eau.* In exploring an alternative sensual realm, Béjart used costumes of vivid color: orange, green, fuschia, lavender, and pink for dancers parading in leotards with matching boas .

Movement supplemented costume, lighting, and verbal text recited on loudspeakers:

> Qui aimes-tu le mieux, homme énigmatique;
> dis, ton père, ta mère, ta soeur, ou ton frère?
> "Je n'ai ni père, ni mère, ni soeur, ni frère."
> Tes amis?
> "Vous vous servez là d'une parole dont le
> sens m'est resté jusqu'à ce jour inconnu,"
> Ta patrie?
> "J'ignore sous quelle latitude elle est située,"
> La beauté?
> "Je l'aimerais volontiers, déesse et
> immortelle,"

L'or?
"Je le haïs comme vous haïssez Dieu."
Eh, qu'aimes-tu donc, extraordinaire étranger?
"J'aime les nuages...les nuages qui passent,
Là-bas...là-bas....les merveilleux nuages." [73]

Who do you love, enigmatic man,
Your father, mother, sister, or brother?
"I have no father, mother, sister, brother."
Your friends?
"You use a word, the sense of which to this day has no meaning."
Your country?
"I don't know its latitude?"
Beauty?
"Well, then, I would accept it gladly,
immortal goddess."
Gold?
"I despise riches as you despise God."
What do you like, remarkable stranger?
"I like the clouds, the clouds going by.
There, over there, the marvelous clouds."

In Béjart's staging of this work, an effect of collage reminiscent of Baudelaire's theory of *correspondances* is maintained. Béjart enhances the connection of the senses by wafting a perfumed mist onto the circular stage space of the Palais des Sports in Paris. There dancers with starkly-colored boas (fuschia and exotic pink) objectified the erotic intensity of the lyric performing five entertwining *pas de deux* creating elaborate improvised forms. Their movements were counterbalanced by a second group of dancers clothed entirely in black who performed physically invoking the visual presence of an echo. Enacting through movement the double of scenic action, both groups revolved in counterpoint, concurrent with the counter-clock-wise revolving motion of the stage. The result, causing a continuous shifting perspective of plastic form,

---

73 Charles Baudelaire. " L'Etranger." In *Petits Poèmes en Prose* (Paris: Garnier-Flammarion, 1967), 33.

forecasts at random intervals, static poses coupled with the creation of intricate shapes that, while constantly changing, nevertheless were static at random points onstage. To the spectator, Béjart's conception of *Baudelaire* invokes a random fluidity of thematic content suggesting corresponding polarities of color, movement, and tone, resplendent of Baudelaire's dominant theory of the correspondence of varying sensual effects.

As prototype of the literary ballet, *Baudelaire* claims as its legacy an extreme fluidity of form achievable on multiple levels of representation. Yet, in the ballet *Serafita/Serafitus* (1974), based on the tale by Balzac, Béjart further develops the form of literary collage begun in *Baudelaire*. This second distinctly "literary" ballet differs from *Baudelaire* in that Béjart returns to the stage for the first of several appearances as performer, enacting logocentrically the character of father/master of ceremony within his own artistic creation. Through his portrayal of the father, a character link between the dream and reality sequences of Balzac's tale is revealed that is reminiscent of techniques of Symbolist stagings. As a device with which to signify the presence of the interior realm of spirits, Béjart uses a loudspeaker. Thus, through the use of the monologue, the voice of the *metteur-en-scène* is both an affective element, designed both to create and to dominate action on stage logocentrically, yet also to fulfill the dictates of narrative. Béjart has said of his own improvised participation:

> I do not intend to dance anymore and when I did the ballet, it was not intended that I should be onstage. But when I saw the ballet, I realized something was missing....In the novel, the father is the older person, and if you cut the father from the tale, it's meaningless. And so I realized with the three people on the stage...the boy, the girl, and the angel...that the central figure is missing. That is why I put myself on the stage. [74]

---

74 Personal Interview: Maurice Béjart, 1978.

The performance of the work was Béjart's earliest attempt to portray a major literary theme of the Romantic period. Based on the work from Balzac's *La Comédie humaine,* the tale owes its principal theme to the theories of Emmanuel Swedenborg, a Swedish mystic and philosopher who believed that angels communed with mortals on earth. Its sources were gleaned the early 1820s, a period when Balzac was interested in religious study. In 1914, the Irish poet William Butler Yeats wrote how Swedenborg:

> affirmed for the modern world or against the abstract reasoning of the learned, the doctrine and practise of the desolate places, of shepherds and of midwives, and discovered a world of spirits where there was a scenery like that of heart; human forms, grotesque or beautiful, senses that knew pleasure and pain...all that could be painted on canvas or put into stories to make one's hair stand up .

> All angels were once men and it is therefore men who have entered into what he calls the Celestial State and become angels and who attend to us immediately after death and communicate to us their thoughts. [75]

In *Serafita/Serafitus,* Béjart captures through staging the spiritual quality of the Balzac tale and uses as his tools internal monologue juxtaposed against a skillful alternation of set design. Situated at the dawn of the 19th century, *Serafita/Serafitus*, by Honoré de Balzac, recounts the story of an angel's descent to earth. A young Norwegian girl, Minna, is sure she is in love with a strange creature who is known as Serafitus. The angel, in turn, tells her he is not for her. Similarly, Wilfrid, envisioned by Balzac as a young knight, is in love with a mysterious Serafita who tells him, in like manner, that she is not meant for him. Minna and Wilfrid discover, at the end of Balzac's tale, that their love for this distant creature is unreal. The inaccessibility of divine love is revealed to them through the presence

---

75 Lady Gregory. Quoted in *Visions and Beliefs in the West of Ireland.* (New York: Oxford University Press, 1970), 312.

of an androgynous angel, so that each may discover their love for each other. For Balzac's nordic setting for the tale, revealing Swedenborg's love for desolate places, Béjart conceived a stage *décor* resembling glacial blocks of ice. For the spiritual dialogue between mortal and angel, two tall Renaissance statues of angels evoke the celestial setting of a divine realm.

Balzac fashions the character of Minna as an innocent and pure young girl and depicts Wilfrid as a troubled young knight who dreams only of conquering the world. His principal protagonist, Serafita/Serafitus is based on the character of Falthurne, the magician. Taken from his first novel, this character symbolizes the combined virtues of knowledge and of power. In the tale, a mystical realm is described,

> Une matinée où le soleil éclatait au sein de ce paysage en y allumant les feux de tous les diamants éphémères produits par les cristalisations de la neige et des glaces...deux personnes passèrent sur le golfe...vers le sommet duquel elles s'élevèrent de frise en frise. Etait-ce deux créatures, était-ce deux flèches? Qui les eut vues à cette hauteur les aurait prises pour deux eiders cinglant de conserve à travers les nuées. [76]

> In a morning where the sun burst its light in the heart of this countryside illuminating fires of all ephemeral diamonds produced by crystallization of snow and ice...two beings passed over the gulf toward the summit from which they glided from peak to peak. Were they creatures or arrows? Whoever saw them at this height would have mistaken them for two eider ducks steering cautiously across the clouds.

Béjart stages the mystical realm of the Norwegian *fjords* exhausting the possibilities of narrative through his interplay of three distinct *mises-en-scène*. Of these, backdrops of rocky cliffs frame the

---

[76] Honoré de Balzac. "Serafita/Serafitus," *La Comédie humaine*. (Paris: Seuil, 1966), 129

principal two *pas de deux* that are danced by Serafita/Serafitus with Minna and Wilfrid, respectively.

The role of the angel, Serafita/Serafitus is skillfully performed by Ivan Marko. The gauze-like texture of the angels' wigs and the costumes composed of leather tunic and shield recall an idyllic feudal realm inhabited by teutonic knights. In contrast to these primary *décors*, a third, opposing the banal to the realm of the imagination, portrays a ballet classroom. A stylistic device, this third setting, allows Béjart to control stage action through the imposition of multiple *mises-en-scène*. The multiplicity of settings onstage deflects the audience's point of view. The regard of Béjart as *metteur en scène* is enlarged by the audience's gaze subsuming his point of view as their own. The opening stage image is allegoric: a single figure adorned by opulent orange brocades lowers himself, head downward, onto the stage. Descending on a long singular rope, accompanied by a loud sonorous throb lasting several minutes, the figure, an angel, places a crown centerstage. This action in turn is followed by the recitation of the first of four *auteuristic* monologues which frame the interior narrative. Their recitation creates a separate element or layer of time which fuses together the time frames of literary text and onstage action.

In the first monologue, the voice is that of the dreamer who speaks and describes the poet-creator's realm:

> Hier soir, je réalisais Henry Miller,
> Qui me parlait de quelqu'un
> Qu'il s'était recontré
> Qu'il ne pouvait empêcher aimer
> Car, cet individu lui avait offert
> Serafita de Balzac.
> J'aime ….regarder les danseurs au travail
> Leur fatigue leur donne des ailes
> A travers leurs port de bras
> Ou la transpiration brise
> J'aperçois
> Les états angéliques

93

Qui habitent en eux.
Comment représenter l'esprit romantique
Irréel, féerique, écrit par Balzac?
Je suis comme chaque jour
En scène de théâtre
On repète
Décore
Nu ou habillè
Les choses du décor: tulle, toile, costume;
Un peu de silence;
Un ange passe....et Mozart.[77]

Yesterday, I read Henry Miller,
who spoke to me
Of someone he had met,
Whom he could not help but like, because
This person had given him *Serafita/Serafitus* of Balzac.
I love to watch the dancers at work.
Their fatigue gives them wings
Through their *port de bras*
Where their perspiration glistens
I perceive their angelic states.
How to represent the romantic, feerique spirit described by Balzac?
I am everyday onstage;
We rehearse, decorate, dressed or undressed;
Elements of décor: net, canvas, costume
A little silence;
an angel passes...and then, Mozart.

At this juncture in the ballet's development, the elocution and phrasing of the omniscient narrator allows a second sequence of action to be evoked through the music of Mozart. Yet this strangeness of mood brought into play by the primary poetic sequence of the opening monologue gives to the work its charm and engages the audience's attention.

---

77 Maurice Béjart. *Serafita/Serafitus* First monologue. Performed Brussels, November, 1974. Translation mine.

In the second scene, following the angel's descent onto the stage a second time, dancers appear as "themselves," performing in white leotards and tights a slow, almost motionless, combination of danced scenes to evoke "center exercises" of the daily class. Dancers perform these movements in silence, creating, along with the Mozart musical passages and interior monologues, a third aural resonance of suggestion.

While dancers command the scenic space, Béjart, as the silent ballet master and magician, sits at stage left on a long couch observing the performance of the class. Seemingly unconscious of his presence the other figures continue their movements as though entranced. He gestures silently as though he were directing them. Against a décor of glittering, pendulous shapes that hang or stand motionless, dancers move in silence in slow motion, giving a surreal effect to onstage action. The sofa on which the magician/director sits motionless is transformed into a heavenly setting.

In intricate spacial designs, Béjart uses choreography in *Serafita/Serafitus* to heighten versatility of dance form by interspersing steps from a *barre* with acrobatic steps performed with a rope and male point work danced by Ivan Marko. Dancers who personify both feminine grace and masculine virility, with their unlimited flexibility and movement range, work together to depict the character who is at once masculine and feminine. Marko attains two textures by using high extensions and subtle variance of gesture. In the sequence of recited text, Béjart turns from the dream world to speak evenly-paced phrases concerning the metaphysical construction of dance. He uses dance as a symbol for heavenly creation throughout the ballet. As Béjart articulates the text, he dissects and unites the performance.

In the second sequence of text, the subject shifts from the analogy of dream and celestial realms to Balzac's original story .

Serafita/Serafitus: <u>Deuxième tableau</u>
Un ballet raconte une histoire, ou bien quelques mots,
des mouvements, des impressions,

comme un carnet de croquis,
Une mille neuves peintures.
Serafita/Serafitus: deuxième tableau

Wilfrid est un jeune homme.
Balzac en fait une espèce de Bonaparte.
Il rêve de conquérir le monde.
Il aime Serafita.
Au fond, c'est un faible.
Il a besoin de protection.

Serafita/Serafitus: <u>Second act.</u>
A ballet tells a story; or at least several words,
Of movements , impressions,
A sketchbook,
A thousand new drawings.
Serafita: Second act.

Wilfrid is a young man.
In him, Balzac creates a replica of Bonaparte
He dreams of conquering the world.
He loves Serafita.
At the base, he is weak and
Needs protection.

Here the narrative text provides context through poetic dialogue that is sensual and replete with metaphor. In the ballet, décor, costume, and movement style of the dancers-in-classroom contrast with the ornate filmed projections of Balzac's principal characters, of angels who commune with mortals.

In his conception of *Serafita/Serafitus*, Béjart enlarges the scope of his use of metaphor and engages it in the processes of the performance itself. The dancers-in-classroom perform in bare feet whereas the three protagonists: Wilfrid, the angel Serafitus, and Minna, wear point shoes. Contrasting the symbols of angel and mortal stresses the dialectic of earthly and heavenly. As a relatively short work whose performance requires less than a full evening, *Serafita/Serafitus* excels as one of Béjart's more tightly developed literary ballets and illustrates the multi-facetedness of his theatrical language and heritage.

In the category of "experimental" works, Béjart's ballet *Stimmung,* developed in alliance with German composer, Karlheinz Stockhausen, exhibits a collaboration of dancer and orchestra. United by a common attraction for the Orient, Béjart and Stockhausen realized *Stimmung* in the early seventies as a work for eleven dancers with orchestra. His collaborative works with Stockhausen reveal Béjart's beliefs that voice enhances dance.

Composed as a musical score for six voices, *Stimmung* relies on the voice's interpretive function with regard to specific movement poses. In *Stimmung,* gestures and movements draw from the "chance dance" theories of Merce Cunningham and had the salutary effect of loosening the choreographer's control over the dance.[78] Movements were improvised individually as each dancer drew from the group consciousness onstage before detaching from their midst. "Sometimes", Béjart explained, "a movement of an arm would be performed in isolation, separate from that of the rest of the body. The same would also be true of the head, and even of the eyes." [79]

Stimmung relied heavily on mathematics. In this ballet, created for ten dancers plus a mysterious eleventh (named in the program notes, *celui qui passe*), Béjart used ten as the "perfect number." Thus, each section of the experimental work depends on a movement pattern containing ten dancers. Béjart liked the effect, the *tetrakis*, a geometrical arrangement of ten elements that represented one of the fundamental problems of the mathematical universe. This formation occurred at both the beginning and during the finale of the ballet.

In *Stimmung,* facial expressions created the ambiance of a room where one meets, experiences, smiles at, or rejects one's companions, all the while going one's own way. The dancers were

78 Sally Banes, *Writing Dancing in the Age of Post-Modernism* (Wesleyan University Press: New England, 1994), 103.
79 Personal Interview: Maurice Béjart, 1978.

free to improvise through a selection of individual gestures as well as the length of time chosen for their execution. The singers also enjoyed this same freedom to improvise, making the work collaborative through its use of different mediums.

The collaboration of Béjart and composer Karlheinz Stockhausen produced a work of considerably smaller scope entitled *Inori* (prayer) that was performed in Paris and later London. Created as a solo for dancer with orchestra, the work lasted a little over one hour. It was created for Béjart himself, who declined the invitation of the composer to perform the work's principal role. Béjart comments during an interview:

> When Stockhausen came to me, he explained that the work would take three weeks of rehearsing. But, when I saw the score, I saw it was actually three months work, if you want to do it well. I said to him that I could not leave the company and, secondly, that I thought it was the wrong thing to do. You see...Stockhausen had made an experiment; he had written every movement in the score. So I told him, even if I do this, I would not be the ideal interpreter.

> I told him I am not against the basic idea of returning to the stage, only no one in the public will believe it's true. As an example, if I should write the music for a ballet and ask Lennie Bernstein to conduct, no one will believe I wrote the music. They will think it comes from Bernstein! "And so," I said to Stockhausen, "if I do this everyone will believe it's my own idea and it will be wrong for your work, because you made everything." And so, he agreed that it was impossible. [80]

Béjart would later state that Stockhausen should have been able to use a classically trained Japanese Nō actor for the work, one who could read occidental music, concluding that, for it to be performed well, the musical score should be learned by heart as well as creation of gestures that are both precise and symbolic.

---

[80] Personal Interview: Maurice Béjart, 1975.

98

As a symphonic work, *Inori* was created for a grand orchestra where, from a podium in the center, a dancer would stand almost motionless. The action on stage would consist of exaggerated gestures of prayer that would, in turn, be indicated on the score. Although the lyrics of *Stimmung,* originally created for the Collegium Vocale of Cologne, focused on names of various deities, the gestures of *Inori* were based on thirteen forms of prayer of different world religions. The length of time, the intensity, and the position of each individual gesture could be read and subsequently performed by the dancer whose musical score was essentially the same as that used by musicians of the orchestra.

On this score, the gesture to be performed was indicated by a number, ranging from "1" to "13." The number appeared on a musical line above the melody line. Successively, the lines written below the melody line indicated numbers from "5" to "60." These symbolized the intensity with which the gesture should be performed as well as its distance away from the body. (Thus, "609" would indicate a projection as far as possible away from the body, whereas "5" would indicate a position with the upper limbs held close to the chest.)

Conversely, a second line below the melody line contained numbers from "3" to "12." These resembled positions of the hands of a clock. (Thus, "3" would indicate the position of three o'clock, indicating, in turn, a right angle to the central weight of the body).
The dancer performed the score of Stockhausen by simultaneously reading the melody and numerical indications. Béjart is quoted as having said, "I am too old to perform on the stage," to which Stockhausen is said to have replied, "To the contrary, you are too young." [81]

It is through experimental development in works such as Béjart's first ballet to electronic music, *Symphonie pour un homme seul* (1959), and the Stockhausen collaborations, that the

---

81 Martine Cadieu, "Plein Feu sur Maurice Béjart," 19.

choreographer presents a task as pretext for staging. A protagonist or group of protagonists must then accomplish the task as a pretext to perform. *Stimmung* introduces simple movements stemming from everyday games, like skipping rope or playing jacks, as a kind of communication. The task of the eleven dancers is to examine their freedom that can function as an obstacle to self-understanding. A mirror placed so that the dancer may gaze at his reflection further symbolizes this obstacle. If in *Stimmung* Béjart has disciplined his will, in *Symphonie pour un homme seul*, he has struggled and exerted himself to achieve it. In *Symphonie*, long black ropes sharply define a stage backdrop as a means of exit. The dancer's task, made real by the elaborate *décor*, is simply to escape.

In the eighties, Béjart proceeded from a mixture of experimental, operatic, and literary forms toward more personal, autobiographical works. *Notre Faust; Wien, Wien, Nur du Allein,* and *Golestan* are part of this group. Sometimes the personal framework of a ballet is concealed, for others it is shown more overtly. In *Golestan,* created in Tehran, Iran in 1973, the Persian poet, Saadi's *The Flower Garden* provided inspiration for Béjart. Composed concurrently to Béjart's conversion to Islam, the framework of this ballet is religious. The symbolism of the ballet derives from the following inscription:

> What can a basket of flowers avail thee?
> Pluck but one leaf from my flower-garden:
> A rose can thus continue five or six days; but the
> Rose flower must bloom to all eternity. [82]

The ballet's form is that of collage and consecutively uses fragments of staged action to express its theme of a voyager lost in the desert who, envisioning a mirage, is met by a group of travelers.

---

[82] *Golestan* or The Flower Garden. United States premiere, Uris Theater, New York 1977; after *Gulistan.*by Saadi.

Consisting of two danced scenes, one featuring the cunning technique of Suzanne Farrell, the other the *élan* and precision of Béjart's male *corps de ballet,* the ballet commences with a quartet performing traditional Iranian music accompanied by danced segments. The narrative draws loosely from the poem by Saadi: before disappearing into the desert night, the voyager watches each man from a tribe of traveling nomads dance a hymn of the desert. In its first scene *Golestan* carefully balances techniques of lighting with the presence of the *danseur-chanteur* to create the illusion of tempest and of mirage.

In the second scene, dominated by the quick expressive counterpoint of ballerina Suzanne Farrell, spots of light projected onto the stage from above are accompanied by the sound of a whirling windstorm. Together lighting and sound project an aura of intoxication. The frenzy of Farrell's movement, of mirage and dream so essential visually intertwined, also frame a dance which is fraught with images of sirens and of dervishes. Sheets of light project onto the stage to create an illusion of limitless space.

In the Brussels production of the ballet, the role of the mystical Rose was performed by Suzanne Farrell who was partnered by Jorge Donn. One of the few works of Béjart's repertory to merge classical and Eastern folk forms, *Golestan* utilized exaggerated movements of the upper torso common to Eastern dance and blended with these the new refined movements of classical dance.

As spectacle, *Golestan* illustates Béjart's tendency to focus on lighting effects to develop mood. During its European premiere in Florence, Mudraist Misha Van Hoeck performed the role of the voyager. Van Hoeck's used the full range of skills of the Mudrist, delving more deeply into the character than would a dancer with solely classical training, Van Hoeck commenced to utter sounds that rhythmically increased in intensity and volume over a span of several minutes. Their increasing force, coupled with uneven rhythms, suggested a person gasping for thirst. Van Hoeck's gesture was supplemented by choreography that increased the intensity of movement and sound. *Golestan* and other works derived from literature make evident the potential value of *Mudra* as training for a total artistic representation.

As a movement motif, a crescendo of jumps accompanied Van Hoeck's gasps in a scene developed entirely through lighting and sound montage. Staging minimalist gesture with carefully honed suspense and an element of pyrotechnical daring reveal Béjart as a master showman. Loud rhythmic clapping enhances a mood of camaraderie among the male *corps de ballet* and punctuates the tension. Finally, the use of a circle in the opening scene illustrates how Béjart's choreography retains visual interest by shifting from scenes whose primary import is to convey mood to scenes filled with captivating pyrotechnical displays.

In the second act, entitled *La Vision du jardin*, Béjart does not go as far in his use of special effects. In this act, the visual effect of form is actually enhanced by the use of luminescent costumes and choreographic styling. In this act, the plastic form evoked by the female dancer becomes more important. She is posed in *penché-arabesque*, her body inclined at a breathtaking 180 degree angle. She is supported by a partner while another dancer, leaning backward, extends her leg upward in a *battement* parallel to the first dancer's pose. The plastic arrangement of the two poses suggests the fusion of two flower stems, an image that contrasts with those of the desert revealed in the work's first two acts.

In *Golestan*, a pose will be framed within the frail outline of a minaret whose graceful form dominates the stage, freed from all encumbering of scenery. This staging reveals Béjart's penchant for symbolism in *décor*, based on a single element, whether isolated from the context of the ballet or woven within the solos.

Golestan's mise-en-scène consisted of a black curtain contrasting with the white silhouette of a mosque. Nine musicians sat atop a raised stage playing traditional Iranian folk music. Underneath, a smaller mosque, where the color scheme was reversed, created a second frame that permitted dancers to enter and exit the stage at will.

As a creative rendering by Béjart of his personal religious aesthetic, the work achieved its force by the use of dynamic planes of form, lighting, and vocal sound.

In this spectacle work, as in others by Béjart that follow this principle, a single male dancer cast forth a sense of brotherhood that permeated the all-male *corps de ballet*. Through movement that charges forth only to be subdued and later aroused, the surging energy of the choreography, ever unfurling, evokex the spell of a dervish frenzy. Thus, in Béjart's ballets of the seventies and eighties, he revealed a revolutionary dance aesthetic, applying his anarchic conception of *métissage* to create works in which a collage of historical events comprises a narrative of various scenes suggesting questions and dilemmas of the contemporary world.

In a later evening-length spectacle work entitled *Malraux ou le Métamorphose des dieux,* produced in the mid-nineties, these questions were brought forth to surround the personnage of André Malraux as creator of mythologies as well as to elicit response from the spectator. Although not personified onstage, the figure is evoked kaleidascopically by danced scenes where the statesman appears alternatively as writer, pilot, statesman, adventurer, or as chauffeur to Friedrich Nietzsche. In like manner, in the French Revolution bi-centennial commemorative spectacle *Revolution-Evolution*, it is Volange, *l'ami du peuple,* danced by Jorge Donn, who descends on a cord from the ceiling of *Le Grand Palais* to retell to children the story of the Revolution. In the opening scene, numerous clowns drive bicycles onto the stage proclaiming, to violins, a text by Robespierre, *"On a pris la Bastille."* In more recent works such as *Pyramide* (1991) Béjart bases his ballet on yet another event concerning the progression of ancient civilizations: the unveiling of the Louvre Pyramid in Paris. In this ballet, Béjart portrays each of the five civilizations of Egypt as a principal motif. Commencing with images of Egyptian pharoahs, continuing through tableaux of Ancient Greece to scenes of Muslim civilization, followed by images of Napoleon

Maurice Béjart rehearsing Jorge Dunn and Suzanne Farrell, 1974.
Courtesy of Thêatre Royal de La Monnaie.

Maurice Béjart rehearsing Suzanne Farrell, 1974.
Courtesy of Thêatre Royal de La Monnaie.

Bonaparte, Béjart concludes with present-day scenes of contemporary civilization.

Though often interlaced with *clichés* and with themes repeated from earlier works (the encounter of Isis and Osiris, the presence of Dionysus the god, and the mythical aspect of the hero, Napoleon), Béjart's ballets interlace personal vision together with elements of autobiography. As such, they appeal to a variety of viewers, admitting within their corpus the necessity of being true to self, through knowledge directly transmitted from father to son. In *Pyramide,* the mythic father conceived by Béjart is the spirit of a muslim sage who, having died in 861 at Gizeh, initiates a symbolic voyage forward in time.

In recent decades, Béjart's spectacle works have tended to blend the experimental, the literary, and the autobiographical. Evening-length spectacles such as *Don Giovanni, Notre Faust,* and *Révolution/Evolution,* the result of experimentation, yield a hybrid form possessing a distinctive personal signature. In works so chronologically diverse *as Le Molière imaginaire* (1977) and *Mozart Tango* (1990), Béjart's fascination with systems of stage effects has led to creating *mises-en-scène* that are at once dynamic in character, yet jarring to the senses. One example is the *barre* used as a point of regard, from the stage to the spectator and back in such works as *Dichterliebe.*

Critic Michael Kirby wrote of Béjart's early staging of Aristophanes *The Birds,* as being performed in a circus ring with dancers speaking lines of dialogue. According to Kirby, Béjart's choreography contains many examples of dance coming far closer than in previous decades to the realm of total theater.[83] One example of this "total theater" is *Notre Faust,* Béjart's evening-length spectacle work discussed in Chapter I. The ballet proceeds through a fusion of literary collage and operatic form, and develops, through a series of tableaux, scenes that are vivid and autobiographical. Béjart returned

---

83 Michael Kirby, ed. "Creative Staging: A Key to Total Theater," *Total Theater,* (New York: E.P. Dutton, 1969), 128.

to this form with *La Mort subite*, a work choreographed in the late eighties in which he symbolically recreated onstage his relationship with his father, Gaston Berger. *La Mort subite*, set in a cafe in Brussels, becomes the scene of multiple encounters with Jean Vilar, Weiland Wagner, and other personalities of the theater. This ballet also depicts symbolically his own last encounter with his father as he has stated in an interview:

> C'est la mort subite de mon pêre, et c' est la mort dans ce qu' il y a de plus inexorable et, en même temps le plus beau; parce que je crois que la mort subite c'est le champ dont on rêve. [84]

> It was my father's death, a case of death at its most inexorable and yet at its finest hour, for I believe that we all aspire to a sudden death.

Béjart's statement also reveals his sense of obligation to dream and to see in the very act of dreaming an element of truth. For Béjart, the father, Gaston Berger, symbolizes both the choreographer's union with and severing from his past. Béjart's more contemporary ballets concern two principal landscapes: the envisioned union with the father and the mystical temple. These landscapes provide the setting of such spiritually autobiographical works as the ethnically-based *Golestan* and *Pyramide*. And, from the ancient troupe of Molière, Béjart borrows the stage of the circus.

---

[84] Quoted from Jean-Pierre Pastori:. *Maurice Béjart* (Lausanne: Favre, 1992), 39.

CHAPTER FOUR
FIVE DANCERS IN SEARCH OF BEJART

In the late seventies, when I traveled six weeks with the *Ballet du XXième Siècle* on tour for an autumn Paris season at Le Palais du Congrès I observed classes, watched rehearsals and was given the privilege of remaining backstage to observe both dancers and Béjart engage in various stages of class, rehearsal, staging of props and other scenic devices as processes of performance. Subsequent visits to Brussels and to Lausanne, throughout the seventies and mid-eighties, resulted in a kinship with this company. This rare camaraderie was one formed by numerous encounters with choreographer and dancers, at work and at rest. In a history which spans over forty years of European ballet, Béjart has acquired a faithful public. He allows few interviews, however, prefering instead to converse with friends, informally. Knowledge of his past or most intimate thoughts, Béjart reserved for few people.

Béjart carefully chose performance spaces for his only spectacle works. In the city of Paris, these included diverse architectural spaces such as *Le Théâtre de l'Etoile* near the *Arc de Triomphe, Le Palais de Congrès*, and a circular sports complex near the fifteenth *arrondissement*. Béjart integrated their versatility, both in terms of stage surface and parameters, into the framework of danced representation.

Since Béjart's early Parisian seasons in the fifties and sixties and subsequent moves to the cities of Brussels and Lausanne, his style influenced audiences in terms of what they accepted from newer, more modern companies and also their conception of dance itself. In his choice of themes derived from major literary works and in his use of an essentially male *corps de ballet*, his ballets departed from traditionally-conceived themes of classical ballet repertory during these decades. Instead, they conceived dance as a statement of social protest, employing a prestigious array of experimentation in sound, lighting, and décor, and the assigning of the principal role to an ideal male dancer onstage and to an almost exclusively male *corps de ballet*.

Always a city friendly to Béjart, Paris excelled as a place of performance because of its several publics, including those who attended posh season openings, and tourists. Paris offered to performing companies several voluminous stages; in addition, Parisian seasons also served as occasions for Béjart to thank critics who had first applauded him as an artist during his beginnings as a choreographer and performer.

In the mid-seventies, while I was a student at Berkeley researching a senior thesis on Béjart's dance, the choreographer gave me a rare invitation to Brussels and Paris, where I observed performances, rehearsals, and activities backstage during a major repertory season. Béjart's invitation had been accorded following a performance of *Stimmung* at the San Francisco Opera House. *Stimmung* was a stage work choreographed for dancer and orchestra in collaboration with the composer, Karlheinz Stockhausen.

In Paris, a direct route led from La Place de L'Etoile down the Avenue de la Grande Armée to the Palais de Congrès where I was permitted to witness rehearsals and performances of the two main season premieres: *Golestan* and *I Trionfi di Petrarca*. *Golestan's* drama commanded images of mysticism and the Middle East where Béjart had recently traveled. He identified with the central role, created in the ballet by dancer Jorge Donn, of the traveler in quest of chimera, the mystical rose. Representing the dancer as seeker, the ballet enacted the personal metaphor more clearly than if Béjart had spoken to the press of his then-recent conversion to Islam.. During our later interview he stated, "You must put religion at the center of your life." For Béjart, this center had also included the stage as I was to learn during our many visits.

A second performance during this early season in Paris, *I Trionfi di Petrarca*, echoed his feelings about the theater. In the history of his choreography, this ballet typified a taste for opulent, spectacle performance in which traditional forms of classicism and traditional stage settings were forsaken. In turn, they were replaced by a richer mixture of gaiety, strong rhythmic movements, and exaggerated effects, wedding entities of performer and performance. *I Trionfi di Petrarca* was Béjart's first attempt to show onstage the particular type of performer, the *danseur-chanteur* to whom he had given birth.

How much this conception of performance was inherited from Béjart's beginnings in Marseilles or by his experience as a struggling performer in Paris is conjecture. In Béjart's first seasons in Paris' Le Théâtre de L'Etoile, he had performed traditional classical roles in such works as *Les Chaussons rouges* (the red shoes), *Le Songe d'une nuit d'hiver*, and *Les Patineurs* (the skaters). His early performances in two of Paris' smallest theaters by the companies *Les Ballets Romantiques* and *Les Ballets de l'Etoile* tell their own story. Béjart could not become, for the classical stage, the dancer he aspired to be, so he turned to a different kind of performance, known for multiple methods of staging as the Béjart "signature."

A slightly overweight figure who frequently wears black, Béjart is considered by dancers as intense. He often seems unaware of his charisma and his ability to transform the talent of the dancers he directs. He is a private person. A devoté of Islam, he is always close to prayer.

Considering Béjart's company and school, versus his private life, I realized that his devotion to his company overshadowed his personal concerns. He guards the former, keeping a schedule at once exacting and precise. He is most in his element at rehearsals, shielded by the realm of work. *Reculez un peu* (move upstage a little), he calls to dancer Shonaugh Mirk; *plus profond* (higher, higher) he calls to Mudrist Misha Van Hoeck. In the rehearsal hall in Brussels or in the auditorium of the Palais in Paris, his blue eyes rearrange the stage. For him, the stage is a puzzle whose pieces constantly shift from space to space. For Béjart, each ballet, like each dancer, consists of a unique and singular portrait.

In this particular season, Béjart's star performer was Suzanne Farrell, performing her final season before returning to dance with the New York City Ballet under the direction of George Balanchine. Papers announcing the company premieres headlined her presence as *La Belle Américaine de Béjart* (Béjart's beautiful American).[85] People noticed the ballerina wherever she traveled, usually accompanied by her husband Paul Mejia and their dog Duchess. Her performances allowed Béjart to choreograph works for a principal ballerina armed with technical suspense and allowed him to project his artistic itinerary into different theatrical realms. Prior to her tenure, the company had been known as "a company of soloists" with no reigning star.

The backstage area of the *Palais de Congrès* consisted of two floors of dressing rooms in addition to several directly to the rear of the performance space. How Béjart's company appears backstage cannot be described adequately. Onstage all was orderly, arranged, and pristine; backstage, dancers practised at all hours in brightly-lit dressing rooms located on either side of a carpeted corridor strewn with remnants of makeup and props. Classes given separately for men and for women took place in the morning. Frequently these classes were observed by distinguished visitors. Classes concentrated on various aspects of ballet technique, such as difficult *enchainements en diagonale,* combinations of steps usually taught only in classes for men.

In contrast, women's classes focused on endurance. Farrell was readily seen as the gauge through which other female members of the company measured not only themselves, but also their artistic ability. For Béjart, the company always symbolized family; it is a company of dancers whose efforts to work as a team are as important as the talent of any individual star. Farrell, however, was his muse whose presence in his ballets during this season attracted larger than usual Parisian crowds.

---

85 "La Belle Américaine de Béjart," *Journal de Dimanche,* (Paris, Nov. 3, 1974).

During rehearsals, Béjart would sit in the huge cavernous pit below the stage, microphone in hand. *Tout en marchant, descendez le corps!* (as you walk, lower your body), he called to dancers in the ensemble of *Il Trionfo dell' amore*, the first tableau of the ballet *I Trionfi di Petrarca*. Locking their arms, three dancers formed a sinuous succession of steps which represented the trials of love's bondage. *Gardez votre distance, vous êtes trop l'un sur l'autre* (keep your distance, you are too much on top of each other), he would call out again, as dancers Bertrand Pie and Rita Lussi performed the roles of Love and its guardian, the Chimera.

Throughout what seemed one endless rehearsal, Béjart simultaneously controlled diverging patterns on stage while creating and recreating each of the separate parts of a given ballet in his mind. At one point, he explained:

> There are three levels, that is thre *étapes* to my work. The first is the company. I have tried to do very much with the company to obtain something different. Then, with Mudra, I tried to obtain a different kind of actor-dancer who can perform not only dance but also act and sing...then, in a third part of my research, I work on a method to give dance to common people. [86]

Béjart considered each ballet a separate project for research, a separate means of communication to a hitherto unknown public. In Mudra, his school located in the center of Brussels, he had formed artists able to perform different and unpredictable combinations of movement performed simultaneously with vocal gymnastics. With two premieres in four week's time, his sense of urgency was overwhelming. True to his own unique personal style, no one, not even the dancers themselves, were able to predict the form of the dance that would finally appear onstage.

Ballerina Angèle Albrecht communicated during an interview that Béjart needed people who could be many things. Her words

---

78 Personal Interview: Maurice Béjart, March, 1978.

pleased Béjart who seemed willing, during the creative process contained in each rehearsal, to expand her range of performance. During this particular season, in March 1976, Béjart, the writer, emerged. Flammarion had just published his autobiography, *L'Autre Chant de la danse*; a series of paintings by Albrecht was on display at a local gallery. Both the public and private Béjart were onstage.

Béjart's first successes in Paris had preceded this season. In the early fifties, two nascent companies, the *Ballets Romantiques* and the *Ballets de L'Etoile,* in which Béjart as performer had danced and choreographed not only modern but also classical ballets, caused Parisian audiences to return, spellbound. These early companies had performed on a dimly-lit stage and, due to economic constraints of the post-war period, made use of sparse sets. Béjart's staging of *La Symphonie pour un homme seul* was an example through its use of stage *décor* composed simply of thick black ropes suspended from the stage ceiling.

When *La Symphonie pour un homme seul* was created in the mid-fifties, Béjart himself was hardly aware of its importance to his career. At first, he was said to have declared that it was created rapidly, as though through lack of a conscious awareness of the creative process. Devoid of lengthy preparation, and avoiding the parameters of any particular style, Béjart then claimed that his inspiration did not differ from that used in conception of classical works.

Three weeks after the premiere of *La Symphonie pour un homme seul*, enthusiastic critiques had persuaded Béjart to abandon all of his previous Chopin-based repertory, performed since the formation of the company, the *Ballets Romantiques* in 1953. Only three works from this early repertory remained: *La Belle au boa, La Mégère apprivoisée*, and a newer choreography of *Le Songe d'une nuit d'hiver*. Béjart could then concentrate on works of a more experimental vein that would become his signature.

The prime innovation attributed to *Symphonie* was its music: *musique concrète*. Developed by Pierre Schaeffer, then director of

O.R.T.F. [87] as a manipulation of noise and brute sound, recorded and then submitted to a series of electronic manipulations, *musique concrète,* reinforced the sparse set design and heavily-textured, forceful gestures of Béjart's dance. It created new archetypes of man and woman that would be accepted by mid-century European audiences as ballet. In the ballet, the characters of Man, performed by Béjart, and Woman, performed by Michèle Seigneuret, stood entrapped in a maze of vertically hanging ropes. Two distinct lines of choreography opposed each other, then fused, then portrayed in the process of juxtaposition alternating allegories of dominance and desire. Responding to the vivid, rapidly performed, circular arm movements of the woman, the man propels his body against the floor in response to a harsh, repetitive sound. In one movement the woman gyrates, hanging onto the ropes, kicking her legs back and forth above the man held motionless by two persons from a crowd. Evoking a group of strangers who are at once predatory and nameless, the crowd echoes the woman's dance through its own movements. The symbolic power of her dance, composed of sharp kicks and twists that, in their seductiveness, eventually destroy the man, also rid him of his power over her. The tension created derives from the suggestion of fear and anguish resulting from enslavement and from the desire for the unattainable. As the crowd converges on the man, evoking the circular form symbolic of completion, the man flees from their midst by climbing one of the loosely hanging ropes. As the curtain falls, he disappears.

Bejart would write that *musique concrète,* as a signature of this work, was "the utilization of sonorous material as text." [88] Sound can, by its brutality and abrupt contrasts, underscore the validity of verbal text, rendering certain forms of poetry more enduring.[89] One of many scores presented to Béjart by Pierre Schaeffer and his team after viewing a performance of the ballet, *La*

---

87 *Organisation Radio Télévision Française.*
88 Marie-Françoise Christout, *Béjart,* (Paris: Seghers, 1972) 86. Translation mine.
89 Livio, *Béjart,* 47.

Mégère apprivoisée, the electronic music segments of *La Symphonie pour un homme seul* offset previous poor reviews . Once Béjart's company performed this spectacle, it found itself on its way to public acclaim. Produced two years after Beckett's *Waiting for Godot, La Symphonie pour un homme seul* used the same sparse sets and single spotlight as principle stage elements. The performance elicited critical praise and its success established Béjart as a choreographer acclaimed for his daring in all realms of danced experimentation.

As critic Antoine Livio stated, few realized what Béjart faced in his first seasons in Paris in the mid-fifties.90 He would not become a dancer "who succeeded," which is one reason why the particular pathway of his ascent as choreographer assumes importance. The success of *La Symphonie pour un homme seul* was a turning point, causing Béjart to term his apprenticeship the years preceding its production. During this period, two themes emerged which mark his ballets today: one is a preoccupation or reliance on *mise-en-scène;* the other the pivotal relation held with his father, Gaston Berger.

In many of his works, Béjart was influenced by Berger not only as father, but also as mentor and friend. The symbolic father, both wise and nurturing, returns again and again in works such as *Notre Faust* and *Serafita/Serafitus,* discussed in Chapter Two, and in works of the eighties such as *Révolution/Evolution,* and *La Mort subite.* The image of father is thus separate from that of Berger, philosopher.

Béjart would speak of his father as *maître,* one who initiated the child into various rites of discovery. Berger's accomplishments were numerous: in 1949, he had assumed the post of General Secretary of the Fulbright Commission and had begun to create, from scratch, methods of application and proposals for a new university structure. In 1953, he was appointed Adjunct Director and then General Director of the Enseignement Supérieur du Ministère de l' Education Nationale. For Béjart, Berger's image was threefold: the

---

90 In his text Livio frequently cited the poverty of early Parisian seasons and struggles faced by Béjart himself and by members of his company.

self-made man; the father (who, when his son would abandon university studies to dance, could not support him financially); and the philosopher.

In *La Mort subite*, choreographed in 1990, Béjart privileges a fourth image of his father, that of a twin brother. Choreographed by Béjart at age sixty-two, the same age that his father died. this work became, as a process of representation, a justification for his father's life. Its title references the literary cafe in Brussels where the two met for the last time. Béjart reveals a sense of "twinship" with the father in the following passage:

Oui, un frère jumeau. Vous savez, quand on pense aux disparus on les fige à l'âge de leur mort. Ma mère est une tres belle jeune femme de vingt-sept ans. Ma mère est une très jeune femme et je la pense comme ma fille.[91]

Yes, a twin. You know, when we think of the departed, we fix them in our memory at the age of their death. Today I see my mother as a very young woman of twenty-seven years; I see her as my daughter.

In the textual narrative which forms the base for this ballet, Béjart uses Berger's notebooks, illustrating his father's profound influence on his psyche:

C'était quelqu'un qui, à la maison, je me souviens de voir des chinois, des hindoues, les américains du sud, des africains. Mon père, il y avait un fleuve qui coulait entre lui et de differents continents, de la terre rattachée à toutes les cultures.

He was someone who would invite to his home persons from China, India, South America, and Africa. There seemed to be an immense river that flowed from my father to different continents from an earth connected to all cultures. [92]

91 Personal Interview: Maurice Béjart, 1978.
92 Personal Interview: Maurice Béjart, 1978.

A parallel can be drawn between the writings of Berger, the reformer of the philosophy of education, and Béjart the reformer of dance. Berger believed that individual reflection and social organization could culminate in action to produce what he termed "historical." Bejart professed a similar belief in the power of dance to wield onto contemporary culture a unifying agent. In his dream-biography, he would write, nearly a decade after his father's death,

> Aller vers la lumière
> Sortir de ma chambre
> Sortir de la nuit
> Sortir de la forêt
> IL FAUT QUE JE DANSE. [93]

> To go toward the light
> To go out of my room
> To leave the night
> To leave the forest.
> I MUST DANCE.

A classmate and confidante from this early period is ballerina, Violette Verdy. Describing how hard Béjart worked to become a classical dancer, she reflected:

> Maurice was completely sincere insofar as his dedication to ballet as a pure art form was concerned. He wanted to be a classical dancer, then he found out quite quickly he did not have the most ideal proportions nor the most ideal height. It was not just that he was not tall, but that his legs were neither very straight nor long...I am sure it was a source of much personal heartbreak and suffering because I am very sure he was sincere about his work and about being a good dancer. He had a good technique which was very sharp and very clean. [94]

---

93 Béjart, *LC*, 30.
94 Ibid.

Verdy and Béjart had studied together at the studio of Mme Rousanne in Paris. Verdy related how, in Paris, Béjart lived in a little room on the rue Bergère behind the Opera, in a quarter of ill-repute. In his tiny attic, she related:

> You could see the combination of a very pure, idealistic personality combined with that of someone who was a little machiavellian and devilish. All sorts of arts and religions were mixed: a picture of a saint would thus be placed next to something very diabolical; likewise something Oriental might be placed beside something which was westernized. [95]

Even more evident was Béjart's vision of what would come. Béjart imagined a ballet for Verdy to be entitled *Violetta* and to be performed to interlude music from Giuseppe Verdi's *La Traviata*. Eventually, it was danced by another ballerina Claire Sombert. During our interview, Verdy reminisced: "That's when I missed the boat with Béjart." During our interview, Verdy described Bejart's personality as a scenario encompassing the tragicomic, the tender, the touching, and the offensive, describing, at all times, a duality beneath the surface. "During that period, Bejart was expressing in his personality all of the elements that marked him the deepest or strongest."

In Paris, Béjart studied with Leo Staats of the *Paris Opéra*, finding in his teacher a generous taskmaster who often forgot to request the fee for lessons. In 1948, he joined the *Ballets de Paris de Roland Petit* for a brief season before leaving for London to join the International Ballet. After several seasons where he danced such classical ballets as the Tchaikowsky/Petipa collaborations, *Sleeping Beauty* and *Swan Lake,* and the Offenbach/Massine *Gaîté Parisienne*, he left for Stockholm to tour with the *Royal Swedish Ballet.* While in Sweden, he choreographed his first film in which two ballets, *L'Inconnu* and *L'Oiseau de feu,* accompanied a narration. In this film

---

95 Personal Interview: Violette Verdy, 1978.

a tenor Tito Gobbi told of the love of a dancer for a tenor. Rendered as naturalistic cinema, this choreography became Béjart's first cinematic essay.

In Paris, Béjart, accompanied by a small group of nine dancers, would perform in any gala or nightclub that would engage them. In 1953, the newly-formed company, *Les Ballets Romantiques,* gave short performances of a repertory, including ballets such as *L'Etranger, Les Sept Tentations du Diable, and Le Songe d'une nuit d'hiver* in *Le Théâtre de L'Etoile* located near the *Arc de Triomphe.* The small company changed its name to *Les Ballets de l'Etoile* in the following year. Amid the poverty of these first seasons, Béjart read profusely, continuing, in Verdy's words:

> ...to eat dreams like people eat cake. He lived on dreams and, although he was very poor, he visualized his dreams to such a degree you couldn't feel sorry for him. You felt the man was rich...and you knew that it would take years for him the express the full thing. He had such a phantasmagoria about him that there was no doubt he could draw on his dreams for a very long time.
> 96

As a choreography which expanded artistic ranges, the performance of *La Symphonie pour un homme seul* led directly to a career path that would culminate in Brussels. The look of his repertory changed, reflecting Béjart's break with conventional ballet custom and choreography. In 1957, he formed the *Ballets de Paris.* The early repertory of this company included signature works such as *Le Sonate à trois,* based on a play by Sartre, and the works *Juliette* and *Orphée* that balanced literary narrative and abstraction. In *Juliette,* six different scenes featured a different psychological archetype through which the character of Romeo nostalgically remembers his love. They introduced a splintering apart of the female persona, a device that Béjart would introduce in later ballets such as *Dichterliebe* and *Notre Faust.* Yet in *Orphée,* created and performed in 1958, Béjart's

---

96 Ibid.

tendancy to fragment one character into separate personalities is redefined, developing a narrative argument through psychological or sensory dynamics. Playing on its creator's fascination with duality, *Orphée* became Béjart's first full-length spectacle performance.

Psycho-analytical processes of the ballet, added to numerous choreographic possibilities, were all-encompassing as spectacle. These processes included casting the double of *Orphée* as a woman, who interpreted in alternation the roles of Venus and Death. Béjart's tendency to render the psychological visible in *Orphée* was further enhanced by the presence of recorded, electronic sound.

"In being an evening-length work to *musique concrète*, *Orphée* is out on the experimental limb," a critic wrote of the work's London premiere:

> That it is not so tedious as it sounds is a tribute to Béjart's theatrical sense. The myth has been warped into insignificance and both choreography and musical score are thin; nevertheless, the gurgling noises merging with Rudolf Kufner's *décors* prove what rich ore Béjart is working in. [97]

Béjart's incessant creation of new ballets caused Maurice Huisman to invite him to Brussels in 1959. There, he would recreate, as a signature ballet, Vaslav Nijinsky's famed choreography *Le Sacré du printemps* . "Maurice Huisman asked me if I wanted to produce *Le Sacré du printemps*, so I told him that he would have to hire me to come to Brussels." "Very well," he said, "but we don't have very many dancers." [98]

Béjart produced *Le Sacré du printemps* with dancers from his own troupe, members of the *Western Theater Ballet*, and dancers from Huisman's own theater, the *Théâtre Royal de la Monnaie*. "After having produced *Le Sacré du printemps*," he stated during an interview, "we continued to tour and would reconvene in London and

---

97 *Time*, "Opera: Faustian Scandal in Paris," (March 27, 1964).
98 Personal Interview: Maurice Béjart, 1978.

Paris with the same three troupes. Each company, of course, danced its own work on the same program. In 1960, Huisman proposed that I stay in Brussels to found a major ballet company.[99]

In Brussels, the response of critics to *Le Sacré du printemps* was favorable. *Le Bruxelles Soir* wrote how:

> The backdrops of pagan Russia were mysteriously harmonized with those of the ballet, *Orphée,* as more and more, the young choreographer withdrew from the enslavement of *Sacré* to unite with a lyricism which is universal. Only dancers stripped of all ornament and civility can translate the gestation of primitive cults, the play of rapture which follows the adoration of the earth, and the warrior jousts between rival tribes.[100]

Another facet of Béjart's inspiration was revealed in performances of these early ballets through the interspersion of verbal text as background to situate or proclaim mood, thus allowing a fusion of performative genre. In the Paris première of *Orphée*, written dialogue interspersed with movement patterns offered tonal values to accompany musical phrasings. *Orphée* signaled a new point of departure, serving as signpost for the choreographer's work in the realm of "multi-theater" in theatrical works to come such as *La Reine verte* (1962) and *La Tentation de St. Antoine* (1963).

In *La Reine verte*, the use of a circular stage foreshadowed uses of scenic space attributed to later ballets. In this work, the combat between man and death took place as death, costumed as an actress, attempts to claim her victims. The text explains that, victorious or conquered, the number of her encounters is infinite. Although each combatant supposes himself to be unique, Death continually pursues her victims.

The production of *La Reine verte* at the *Théâtre Herbetot* in Paris in 1962 illustrated Béjart's mastery of principles of *mise-en-scène*. Interpreted by the actress Maria Césarès and the

99 Personal Interview: Maurice: Béjart, 1977.
100 Quoted from *Le Bruxelles Soir,* March 17, 1964. Translation mine.

dancer Jean Babilée, the ballet begins with the dialogue: *Tu es Poète. On va commencer!* (You are the poet. We will begin). The clang of cymbals follows the text to reveal a tri-partite scenic arrangement of dancers juxtaposed with elaborate stage sets. Entitled respectively *Cygne, L'Heure exquise,* and *La Belle,* the three tableaux comprising the ballet represented neither comedy nor tragedy, yet explored three feminine archetypes subsumed within the choreographer's own quest for self definition and exploration.

Throughout the production process of *La Reine verte,* Béjart would create an intensely personal signature. Although drama critics found the dance sequences of the work to be lacking in musicality and gave the work poor reviews, *La Reine verte* nevertheless created a moment of awareness among audiences. Even though Bejart decided not to publish its libretto, causing confusion among members of loyal Parisian audience, he began to work on a second ballet in the same vein, *La Veuve joyeuse,* to premiere in Brussels the following year.

Expecting a danced operetta modeled on the musical score of Offenbach with gradual accelerations of dance, the Brussels public did not expect the latter to portray a stage design exhibiting horrors and atrocities of World War II. By means of documentary filmed segments, lavish sets of the imaginary Marsovian Embassy were juxtaposed with realistic settings of Paris for the lyric, *Maximes,* all designed by dancer Germinal Casado. It was Béjart's intention in this production to shock his audience through encouraging social outcry. Its highlights included such stylistic juxtapositions as the performance of a male can-can with *finale* sung over a mound of corpses. With *La Veuve joyeuse,* Béjart's personal relationship to *mise-en-scène* was established, focusing upon the possibilities of multi-spectacle to evoke empathy with political or historical event. This relationship is expressed through a personal belief on the part of Béjart that the theater, like the Church, is a mystical haven, a realm of transformation. He has thus stated:

> Through my contact with actors and the stage, I have learned very much, but this is not my future. The body of the dancer is

much more important. If I work with an opera singer, it is just to
learn something in a more technical way. Every time I come back
to the ballet from doing work in the theater, my next ballet is
better. [101]

In an interview with French *metteur-en-scène*, Jean Vilar,
during the course of his career, Béjart reaffirmed the importance of
being able to dabble, to come into contact with and refashion or
create anew, the many elements of the stage.

Je ne suis pas écrivain; mais quand j'étais danseur je n'étais pas
non plus danseur... Je suis un peu comme ces gens qui ne sont
pas specialistes qui sont fascinés de toucher à tout. Je ne veux
pas me comparer à un grand, mais je suis un peu comme a été
Cocteau dans le sens que je suis chorégraphe avant tout. .J'adore
la mise-en-scène. J'ai mis en scène des pièces pour Barrault, pour
Césarès. J'ai mis en scène des opéras...Je joue sur plusieurs
tableaux et j'ai besoin toute ma vie d'apprendre, d'apprendre,
d'apprendre. [102]

I am not a writer, but when I danced I was not a dancer. I
ressemble those people who are not specialists but who, at the
same time, are fascinated with everything. I don't wish to
compare myself to a famous person, but I'm a little like Cocteau,
in the sense that, before everything else, I choreograph. I love the
stage. I have staged works for Barrault and for Césarès. I have
staged operas. I involve myself on multiple levels at once
because I have all of my life had a devouring need to learn.

Bejart's own performances as dancer lacked a certain poetic
effect that could make simple steps take wing but, paradoxically,
contained a penchant for "startling theatrical effects."[103] As
choreographer, he included volumes of poetry, recitations of texts by
Racine, and music he professes "to have learned backwards,"
beginning with the *musique concrète* of Pierre Boulez, continuing

101 Personal Interview: Maurice Béjart, 1974.
102 Personal Interview: Maurice Béjart, 1978.
103 "Faustian Scandal in Paris," *Time,* (March 27, 1964), 43.

chronologically backwards to the composers Igor Stravinsky, Hector Berlioz, Gustav Mahler, Richard Wagner, and, finally, Mozart.

Béjart's total spectacle form, which emerged in the seventies, is one that engages the performer in singing, dancing, or speaking, expressing himself with "the totality of means given him by God."[104] The desire to form a total character as a composite of various personality fragments has always been strong for Béjart. Thus the persona of Faust, for example, is associated, as fantasy, to that of Leonardo da Vinci in the ballet *Faust,* choreographed in 1963.

In the first staging of *Faust* performed in Paris in 1964, the sketch and evocation of The Last Supper combines with the "Song of the Rat" from the Berlioz score. The scenario of this first *Faust* revolves around Mephistopheles' promise to show Faust's bestiality in all of its candor. Thus, the refrain of drinkers demanding a song became, for Bejart, an occasion to introduce the popular image of a discothèque. Through parody of the sacred and juxtaposition of personal with popular symbols, Béjart attempted to prove that only by violating a masterpiece could one truly judge its resistance and endurance. "I believe," Béjart remarked, "that the dance is an archetype which transforms itself and takes on different meanings at different epochs. Thus, the *Faust* one sees today is not the *Faust* of Marlow or that seen during the Romantic period."

To Béjart, choreography is a composite art. He has said:

> If I create a ballet on a given work of music, I take a score and I look for motives. Then I dissect it and reduce it into schemes, like making a charcoal or graphic sketch for a particular design in a painting. Then, for an hour or two, I rest before taking up my work again. I believe it is necessary to understand once with one's spirit in an analytical fashion and, the second time, with the entire body. And so, if one doesn't finish each part of the work completely, one loses...either through having a work which is not

---

104 Personal Interview: Maurice Béjart, 1978.

fully-constructed mathematically, or one which is not "sensed"
through being at one with the music. [105]

When the *Ballet du XXième Siècle* first performed as "a company of
soloists" in the early sixties, being able to dance was not enough.
During this period, Maina Geilguld, Tania Bari, Paolo Bortaluzzi, and
Daniel Lommel stood out against a backdrop of performers due to
their unique ability as soloists to bend the rules of traditional ballet
technique to respond as in several diverse media.

    The late sixties foresaw the emergence of the political Béjart.
His involvement with art led to a more political agenda developed
through social themes in ballets such as *L'Oiseau de feu* and *La
Messe pour le temps présent*. In Lisbon in 1968, Béjart spoke out
against Communism angering his sponsor, the Portuguese
government. Later the same year, his company participated in student
riots in Avignon. Generally, Béjart's political stance proceeded from
emotional involvement with a given theme of his choreography. By
the seventies, Béjart's exploration of social consciousness had
expanded to encompass the spiritual. Each creation of a new ballet
seemed to demand, concurrently, a change in attitude toward religion.
"In *Nijinsky, Clown de Dieu*," dancer Dyane Grey-Cullert explained,
"crosses were everywhere; in *Bhakti*, dancers evoked Krishna and
Rhada, gods of Hindu mythology. Now we are waiting for him to try
Africa." [106]

    By the late seventies, an imaginary museum had begun to
emerge from the overwhelming phantasmagoria of Béjart's
accumulated ideas. If today he professes a love for the architect
Gaudi, it is because Gaudi's name has long been associated with
Barcelona, a city where he feels at home. Likewise, he admires
Gustave Moreau and Paul Klée because their usage of color and
design feed into his own ideas on the theater. One may imagine that
Béjart would like to have been born as Leonardo, since he names the

---

105 Personal Interview: Maurice Béjart, 1978.
106 Personal Interview: Dyane Grey-Cullert, 1974.

child in *L'Autre Chant de la danse* "Leonard" recalling his own imagined childhood in Marseilles.

Because Béjart was fascinated by the Orient, he chose themes dealing with eastern religions for many of his works. To celebrate his own conversion to Islam, he created *Golestan*, stating: "You cannot put religion outside your life. Outside, it is not important. Religion is not meant to be placed outside, but to be in your life. I found in the Orient several essential qualities of human life. To rediscover the Orient is to rediscover the true essence of our being." [107]

During the Parisian seasons that I attended, performances often were followed with dinner at the Marigny. Here, Béjart and his principal dancer, Jorge Donn would mimic a recital of Harpo Marx while playing on a grand piano. Later, during this season, receptions took place at Béjart's apartment on *la rue de la Fourche* in Brussels. The *décor* of this apartment reflected the spiritual life of the choreographer. In contrast to his Parisian apartment, the Brussels apartment was more sparsely furnished. Located on the second story atop a wooden staircase, it seemed a retreat that Béjart jealously defended and where he savored moments shared only among close friends.

In an empty space designed for religious meditation, on a cloth of maroon velvet, lay a Koran. In the living room, framed by magnificent wooden beams and stained glass, portfolios of Japanese lithographs, a tambourine, chips of colored tile, and miscellaneous letters lay scattered on oddly-assembled tables. In a blue folder, a manuscript entitled *En Moi, plus que Toi* (In me, more than you) lay beside a signed copy of *Lettres d'hivernage* (Winter correspondence) by Senegalese poet, Léopold Senghor. The inscription, addressed to Béjart, read, *Car la Danse est le premier art, et l'éssentiel* (Because dance is the first and essential art). [108]

Remaining as yet unclassifiable, Béjart's ballets today await rediscovery, like this abode in Brussels wherein each corner

---

107 Personal Interview: Maurice Béjart, 1977.
108 Léopold Senghor, *Lettres de l'hivernage*, (Paris: Seuil, 1972) 34.

possessed its own particular characteristic or atmosphere. Each choreography explored a separate metaphor, yet drew from the cumulation of all his previous ballets attempted before. The ascending staircase in Brussels suggested a metaphor, eliciting rapports with successions of ballets; so that, at the highest step beside the quarters where Béjart lived and dreamed, one expected to uncover by chance, the key to their meaning.

FIVE DANCERS

Maurice Béjart's *Ballet du XXième Siècle* had achieved its signature look by the early seventies as a company of soloists. He was the first choreographer to use a ballet vocabulary as a technical base, while challenging a *corps de ballet* of men to new levels of brilliance and stardom. Béjart's creation of *pas de deux* and *pas de trois* segments solely for men paved the way for stylistic innovations by other, more traditional companies, thus changing the aesthetic of ballet for following decades.

How was Béjart perceived by his dancers? The five interviewed in this chapter exemplify the individuality and spirit of the company as it existed in the seventies. They were solo performers who enjoyed applause in virtually all world capitals where the company performed. For each dancer, Béjart's company served as a major point of departure toward growth and individual freedom.

In the studio behind the Midi train station, close to the Arab quarter of Brussels the *Ballet du XXième Siècle* revolved in a dawn to dusk rhythm, working continuously within the walls of Mudra. Its studios offered classes in such diverse subject areas as vocal percussion; its small room, one flight above the canteen, offered a spot for meditation; its courtyard, with yet another set of stairs, led to rehearsal halls. Mudra, a haven for dancers, beckoned with activity.

I first met company members during their pre-season tour in Holland. The delicate, serene face of Rita Poelvoorde stared, hidden behind large, shell-rimmed glasses; the freckles of second generation ballerina Monet Robier, daughter of Rosella Hightower, vividly appeared behind a scarf; the frown of Isabelle Babillée, daughter of Jean Babillée, never left her face, even when she performed such humorous ballets as *Ah-vous dirais-je maman*. These performers were studious, engaged in continual experimentation, seeking both to perform and to explore new dimensions for traditional balletic art form. In Holland, I spoke with two young performers, Shonaugh Mirk and Lynn Glauber, before rehearsal, two dancers then referred to as Béjart's "baby soloists." Shonaugh, trained in the School of American Ballet, graduated from Mudra at the time when emphasis at the school had shifted from classical orientation to performance based on a sound and speech resonation emanating from the torso.

Béjart demanded that artists have knowledge of all the arts: music, dance, and drama. Dancers were enthralled with the Mudra approach. Formerly, students had been required to have training in classical ballet technique before entering Mudra. Béjart's company continued to spotlight dancers of high technical accomplishment despite the look of a repertory that featured intricate stagings, *à terre* movement, intricate spacial relationships of scenic elements, and close relationship of movement to narrative. Lynn Glauber, an American who had grown up in Paris, was one of the few non Mudra-trained dancers who commanded many solo roles. One of the youngest classical soloists, she possessed, in the words of a fellow dancer, *les jambes d'une ange* (the legs of an angel).

In contrast, Shonaugh Mink had profited from both schools. Her experience in modern integration of the arts, as espoused by Mudra, caused her to emerge as the model Béjart dancer. Béjart's consciousness of the look of his company, created by the dancer onstage, was apparent. Angele Albrecht and Catherine Verneuil, mature soloists of the period, and younger dancers Lynn Glauber and Shonaugh Mirk, all performed with an attack approach, inherited from their unique composite training. Although choreographer and company were entities apart, dancers who trained with Béjart from that period incorporated technique derived from Mudra training.

Their blended technical approach to dance came to symbolize the unique style of the company.

As these Béjartian soloists performed throughout Western Europe, they punctuated their stage appearance with rare qualities of expression. These solo performers and others who had danced with Béjart returned to their former companies as stronger dancers whose performances defied description. Even seasoned ballerinas, such as Suzanne Farrell, were able to broaden their vast artistic range through performing with Béjart's company.

ANGÈLE ALBRECHT

An early-appearing soloist with The *Ballet du XXième Siècle* who performed as principal dancer in works of the sixties and seventies, dancer Angèle Albrecht embodied onstage the look of Béjart's archetypal woman. In *Dichterliebe* and and in *I Trionfi di Petrarca,* her dramatic portrayals of symbolic feminine archetypes, such as the Woman in White and the object of *Il Trionfo dell'Amore*, proffered dramatic characterizations harbouring both power and intensity. Like many Béjart soloists, her background was classical. Angèle's father had been an accomplished painter; her aunt a singer. She commenced her studies at age six by drawing and painting ballerinas. "I wanted to be a dancer," she said, "and felt if I had a talent, someone would see it. Dancers make a ballet. It's not just a good choreographer. It depends on dancers. It's a shame, in America, everything seems to be based on technical perfection. In Europe, it is more on character." [109]

As a child, Angele's talent earned her seven years of free classes at the Edwardova School in Munich. It prompted the Russian choreographer Gsovsky to offer praise to Angèle's mother concerning the talent of her "little boy" when Angèle was nine. Angèle laughingly explained that, with her short cropped hair, her narrow

109 Personal Interview: Angèle Albrecht, 1977.

hips, and her very broad shoulders, she was indeed boyish, looking like an elementary school child.

After studies in London with the Royal Ballet, Angèle Albrecht danced with Peter Van Dijk at the Hamburg Opera. It was there that George Balanchine noticed the young ballerina and gave her roles in *Concerto Barroco*, *Symphony In C*, and *The Four Temperaments*. In spite of Balanchine's attentiveness, Angèle preferred Béjart from the beginning. She stated during our interview at her home in Brussels, "Although Hamburg gave you a lot of Balanchine, I had wanted since a very young age, to dance the stock Béjart roles of *La Symphonie pour un homme seul*, and *Sonate à trois.*"

Angele's chance to dance with Béjart had commenced with her interpretation of the role of *la femme* in *Nijinsky, Clown de Dieu*. "This ballet," she continued, "was a total *image double* ballet. "Béjart needs people who are many things," she sighed, "One must be able to sing and to dance the 'Black Swan *pas de deux*' simultaneously, if necessary. It is interesting how he starts with people who do one thing in a given ballet, and causes them to do many." Forthright, Angele showed to me during our visit a series of brightly painted tableaux.

"These (pointing to seascapes) were painted by my grandmother," she stated, "and these (pointing to abstractly painted canvases containing blue and red brush strokes) were painted by my father, and these," she said, (pointing to two unusually vivid surreal portraits), "were painted by me." The latter two portraits were of Béjart, who had rejected them for a Paris opening, professing not to approve of their color. One, painted in shades of black and forest green, showed Béjart carressing the feathers of a giant swan with his left hand while another swan, on his right, whispered in his ear. In the background stood three smaller swans whose heads resembled three of Béjart's dancers: Jorge Donn, Michèle Seigneuret, and Germinal Casado. In a second portrait, a group of dancers are overshadowed by a vision in the stomach of a central figure, of blood gushing downward to form the shape of a flag. Below the flag, resistance soldiers fight. Béjart, whose portrait is depicted, stares, his blue eyes glaring, all the while revealing a message of hope.

Commenting on the short ballet *Cygne*, choreographed in the early sixties, biographer-historian Marie-Françoise Christout reveals the choreographer's fascination with swans:

> Tired of seeing ballerinas monopolize aerial movement, Béjart, received an inspiration while reading a poem of Tagore. He dreamed of a flock of swans whose wings beat rebelliously in the evening. To the sound of Indian music, he choreographed the movement of Swans, Paolo Bortoluzzi and Germinal Casado, for Béatriz Margenat. Casado's eyes were made to appear larger by make-up; his cheeks were drawn in, and accentuated an enigmatic vision of swans, flapping their wings. [110]

Illustrating the hypnotizing power held by Béjart over his dancers, *Cygne* was perhaps the first ballet in which men performed aerial movements hitherto given a ballerina. These aerial movements performed by male dancers are today principal components of Béjart's style that relies upon the presence of a male "brotherhood" instead of the traditional female *corps de ballet*.

Painted in blue hues, the second portrait framed a Buddha figure, seated in the lotus, bearing three heads representing the philosopher Nietzsche, the composer Wagner, and the poet Baudelaire. Bearing female breasts that split above the stomach over which are positioned the portrait that is Béjart's, hands in the pelvic area of the figure clutch dancers that struggle to perform as marionettes who cannot escape their strings.

For Angèle, the portraits depict Béjart as he was then known by dancers, as possessing a special combination of qualities: Friedrich Nietzsche's belief in a God who could dance; Richard Wagner's romanticism and love for grand theaters filled with thousands of people; and Baudelaire's fine-line between good and evil illustrated

---

110 Christout, *Béjart* (Paris: Seghers, 1972).

by the *poète-flaneur* who opposes and reconciles opposite sensual extremes. The mood of this portrait recalled the statement made by dancer Violette Verdy during our interview, that there was in Béjart at all times a composite figure, a duality at least, that he was only now capable of expressing, through his dancers.[111]

Remembering these portraits, I was reminded of comments from company members, such as "We are successors of the Cuévas," recalling the period prior to the company's first American tour. "But Maurice," a dancer overcome with anger cries out, "We do it all for you!" To most of the company members, Béjart's presence was one of supreme benevolence; yet to others, it was controlling. A younger soloist, Monet Robier, declared that she would rather dance in the streets than not dance with Béjart. For others, Béjart's company was both the beginning and the end. Angèle Albrecht and her partner Daniel Lommel, came to Béjart after achieving tenure in smaller prominent companies such as the *Ballets Hamburg* and the *Ballets de Paris de Roland Petit*. Whether drawn by his charisma or by their own desire, they felt that their association with the company offered a personal encounter with the mind of its creator.

DIANE GREY-CULLERT

Diane Grey-Cullert joined the company in Paris in 1969 after performing a series of guest appearances in the highly eclectic *Neuvième Symphonie*. One of the first ballets to use nude-colored leotards as principal costuming and one of the first to be set on a circular stage, *Neuvième Symphonie* sold out to packed audiences at the *Palais des Sports*.

Diane had lived "up North," as she then called Sweden. She described her past as replete with "trashy things", such as endeavoring to secure a doctorate to obtain working papers. She had performed in a Swedish version of *West Side Story* and had appeared

111 Personal Interview Violette Verdy, 1978.

at The Royal Swedish Opera opposite Danish *danseur* Erik Bruhn. She arrived in Paris as the result of a telephone call, just as she had been previously drawn to Sweden.

"I've always gotten jobs by telephone," she laughed. "In Finland, I was modelling clothes for a Nieman Marcus-like department store. Someone heard about me in Sweden and phoned, asking me if I wanted the role of the Black Girl in *A Funny Thing Happened on the Way to the Forum*. I was one of those Village types, so I thought, 'what the hell!' Everything to me is an experience. So I said yes."

In Sweden, Diane had met Birgit Akesson who seemed to her as the Walt Whitman of dance. Akesson was directress of the *Choreographiske Institut* in Stockholm at the Royal Academy where, for Diane, she had produced *West Side Story*. She worked with Birgit who knew Sylvia Waters, who had danced the role of the solo black dancer in Béjart's *Ninth Symphony*. Since Waters had recently returned to New York to work with Alvin Ailey, Diane – through the intervention of Akesson-- had received a phone call from the General Manager of the *Ballet du XXième Siècle*, inviting her to audition in Paris for a single season of twenty performances. "I was the last girl on her list," Diane stated during our interview, "simply because I had come from the farthest point (Sweden) and they would have to pay my way. Therefore, I came to Brussels to audition. There, Béjart accepted me as guest artist."

The following ballet in the season was *Baudelaire*, an evening-length work, presented like a circle in the round at the Palais des Sports. Maurice then offered Diane a role in this daring provocative ballet. As stated during our interview, she told him, "I've never had a rehearsal; I don't know the work." He responded, "It doesn't matter; improvise."

Since some of the dancers thought it might be fun to take modern classes, Diane began to teach. At that point, Béjart suggested she join the company. At the outset, Diane had joined because of the *Baudelaire* ballet. She had stayed in Paris to improvise, or perform the work before they had called her in Sweden to ask her to come again to dance it in Brussels. But the deciding factor was Maurice. Diane liked Béjart; she liked him personally. She confided that she didn't like all of his ballets, but that if he asked, she would tell him so.

Diane explained to me how, from the moment of her audition for *Ninth Symphony*, her friendship and trust for Béjart had grown. Yet she concluded, "Everyone in the company hasn't gotten that from him, but neither is everyone completely forthright."

Diane seemed to understand Béjart best. She had performed roles in signature ballets of early seasons including *Les Noces, L'Oiseau de feu,* and *Le Sacré du printemps*. Her favorite roles, however, were those in which she had been allowed to create her own personality directly into the role performed in the ballet. In the early seventies, she saw herself as "a token black performer," without minding what she termed as tokenism. Her best roles--*Baudelaire* and *Ninth Symphony*--to name two, had allowed her not only to be black, but also to create onstage a presence born of her highly developed technique. To her, Béjart conferred on all of his dancers a liberty to perform born from trust, a liberty to dance as each one chose.

After studying music and dance at the University of Pennsylvania, Diane had gone to Finland with the intent to teach in Helsinki. When she arrived, she stayed, finding in Finland a working acceptance she did not receive in the States. After two years, she had achieved recognition by the Finnish government.

"Do you speak Finnish?" I asked. "Yes," she answered, "fluently. Language is like music; if you can sing, you can learn vowel sounds." Sitting in the canteen at Mudra, Diane recalled the company's first San Francisco performance of *Stimmung*, where I had seen her dance. She told me of the night preceding the ballet *première*, when the company had gone to see the pornographic film, *Deep Throat*. Trying to be serious for the following evening's performance was almost impossible. Even Béjart had wondered why the dancers and singers couldn't keep a straight face.

To Diane, *Stimmung* was meant to be without story and was created to form ambiance. The words introduced by Stockhausen its composer included over thirty names of deities, such as Vishnu, Tangorao, Rhea, Isis, representing world religions. "We were trying to create whatever atmosphere you got from it," she recounted. "No definite rules were made, except to cause the audience itself to sense that atmosphere which we, as dancers, communicated." Each dancer in *Stimmung* had as his objective the completion of a task that would include such components as a particular interior attitude toward time, a perception of his body, and a particular style of communicating.

Stimmung was Béjart's first ballet to contain formal elements derivative of analytical postmodern dance practiced by Merce Cunningham and composer John Cage. In terms of its movement, its particular staging, and its use of mirrors, Béjart had made it uniquely his, a part of his company repertory. To dancers like Diane, *Stimmung* followed the format of earlier works, such as *La Symphonie pour un homme seul*, and was described by her as "an adventure in pure abstraction."

Diane and I spoke of the constantly reappearing religious motifs in Béjart's choreography of the period, replete with themes of death and of reincarnation. She laughed, "The trouble is, it's never the same religion. *Actus Tragicus* and *Nijinsky* had crosses -- there were crosses everywhere! When Nijinsky the dancer was portrayed as being on the cross, angels were descending. In *Golestan*, we went to the Middle East; then, in another ballet, crosses would appear again!" Since, at the time of this interview, Béjart had recently converted to Islam, Diane exclaimed in anticipation, "I can hardly wait for him to discover Africa!"

"What Maurice is trying to do," Diane explained to me during our interview, "is to take the multi-art of the theater and show this through the medium of dance. Instead of movement just meaning dance, Béjart uses all the elements. In *Nijinsky, Clown de Dieu*, circus is present. With Maurice, dance has become popular art. He's taken dance away from the elite and given it to the man who watches television!"

As Diane pointed out, "Béjart has a lot of revolt. He's expressing all elements which have marked him the most; he has such a phantasmagoria within that there's no doubt he will draw on it a very long time. Composite or merely complex, Béjart's dance can't be categorized as one theme or one single type of dance. As choreography, his dance has both disappointments and seminal works. Among these, *Le Sacré du printemps* and *La Symphonie pour un homme seul* stand alone." For Diane, *Baudelaire* was a miniature Mudra that, as a ballet, centered itself on voice in addition to drama and rhythmic instruments. "That's what I saw in *Baudelaire*," she laughed: "Angèle singing *La Traviata* within the context of dance, actually using her own voice. The more Mudra there is, the more Béjart has to work with."

"Why do dancers come to Béjart?" I asked. To this question, Diane responded, "I think they come to work. A lot of men and a lot of strong women have utlized Béjart. Now he's preparing roles for Suzanne." For Diane and many others, the company changed during the tenure of Suzanne Farrell. "When Suzanne Farrell arrived," Diane explained, "we were dancing 'with' her; when Maurice began to use her as a 'departure point,' the company changed."

SUZANNE FARRELL

In Brussels and in Paris of the early seventies, whenever Suzanne Farrell performed, the company made headlines. The French press described her as *La Belle Américaine de Béjart*. Farrell credited Balanchine with first placing her feet on the *barre,* but readily recognized Béjart as the man of the future or prospective dance.

In the mid-seventies after performing with Béjart seven years, Farrell decided to return to New York and departed Brussels amid persistent rumors. Although the conditions under which she had originally joined the company in Belgium were often left to guesswork, one thing was certain: she was elated. Among her last performances with the *Ballet du XXième Siècle* were the roles of Laura in *I Trionfi di Petrarca* and of the seductive Rose in *Golestan*. In both, she was ably partnered by Argentinian principal dancer Jorge Donn. Farrell thought of Donn as the perfect partner and would later invite him to New York to appear in George Balanchine's New York City Ballet as guest.

In *I Trionfi di Petrarca*, Farrell danced in the first *pas de deux*, entitled *Il Trionfo della Castità*. She first appeared onstage, seated on a life-size Florentine chariot, framed against a giant fresco. She resembled a jewel, dressed in a gleaming gold costume, and her presence commanded the stage. Choreographically, the steps of the evening performance were simplified, due to Donn's illness. One sensed the audience knew. Farrell, however, a master technician, added flair to such steps as an *attitude* by extending it to an *arabesque*. With commanding grace, she bowed to the courtly clad figures onstage. A dancer had casually remarked that Béjart had given to Farrell her dramatic style, and that under Béjart's tutelage, the young Farrell had gained expressiveness of form in her face and gestures. At her departure, Béjart is said to have remarked that she was not leaving, but was "going home" to Balanchine. During a fleeting moment backstage in Paris, she had expressed disbelief, wondering if, in the late seventies, America would remember her.

Suzanne Farrell and her husband, Paul Mejia frequently took private class apart from company members. In a smaller studio, Mejia was able to direct Farrell more quickly through combinations of dance movement in an effort to help the ballerina maintain her stunning technique. In Paris, Farrell had teased Béjart about being her partner, and calling him "an excellent partner." During our interview, Farrell declined to tell exactly how she had made the decision to come to Béjart, except to say that a telegram had arrived from Montreal requesting that she join the group. Like Diane Grey-Cullert, Farrell stressed the value of the personal relationship which extended beyond that of dancer to choreographer. For Béjart, Farrell would help create works by blending intricate gesture and mime with technical skill. "I found Maurice to be sincere," she stated of their initial meeting. "I had met him before and even shook his hand. But," she added, "his sincerity impressed me most. When sincerity is there, I can give myself to the choreographer to use me in whatever way he wants." Béjart had seen Farrell perform such standard Balanchine ballets as *Agon* and *Four Temperaments*. Initially, he wanted to do new things with her, developing a choreography along the lines of modern dance. But, to Farrell, variety was the key to contentment. Even Béjart's *Sacré du printemps* wasn't all. "As much as I love it," she stated, "I couldn't do it all my life; the same would be true of *Swan Lake*. In dancing two styles, you realize they complement each other and you grow."

"What do you think you have gained in dancing with Béjart?" I asked. She replied, "I have to say that many people ask me how it's different -- dancing first for Balanchine and then for Béjart. I respond that that's not a fair question because I've changed. I've moved; I live in a foreign country. The basic difference in training between Béjart's and Balanchine's companies does not exist because, if one examines Balanchine's way, many things done the way Béjart prefers are similar."

"What things?" I asked.

"The preciseness, the very fast way of moving. Béjart likes to do things very fast; but he also likes 'slowness,' but most companies never reach the incredibly fast-tempo pace of Balanchine."

"Are classes similar?"

"Balanchine gives the most; he gives you more than you can do, but through that you learn to push yourself. So maybe today you can't do the step, but in a month you can. You always need someone to push you, no matter how much desire you have. Usually it's the choreographer or person you're working for. It doesn't mean that you're lazy; you simply want to please. And," she emphasized, "you improve. And they're happy you're doing the steps their way, so they improve! So have I changed? I say that I'm happy with myself," she smiled.

"It's not that Béjart has changed me into a different dancer. I simply do his ballets my way and with his choreography. I don't want to change; I do want to improve. I have my style, as does everyone," Suzanne reaffirmed as we spoke backstage at *Le Palais de Congrès*. "You can improve and grow, but it's also important to have personality and a body; otherwise you are mechanical. This also applies to classical dancers. *Swan Lake* as well as other classics all the time can be just as acrobatic and mechanical as anything else."

In Brussels, Farrell had donned soft ballet slippers for the first time to dance *Le Sacré du printemps.* She had amazed others with her endurance, whizzing through all thirty-two technically difficult variations of the ballet *Ah vous dirais-je maman.* Her technique had changed the look of the company. In returning to Balanchine, she concluded at the end of our interview, she would be better for having performed several years with Béjart.[112]

"Béjart's ballets *Sonate à trois* and *Le Sacré du printemps* are earthy and temperamental, compared to the standard Balanchine repertory. To a certain extent, I am more involved, yet cannot get carried away. Ballet is an art form very dependent on other people and on stages and on one's partner. I suppose my favorite Béjart role is really Juliet in the ballet *Romeo et Juliette.* To my knowledge, Béjart's choreography of this classic is the only one which uses the Berlioz score. I feel this ballet will never be dated: the costumes are simple and not at entirely of the period, yet they include swords and boots. Visually, the ballet has no century, and in the ending, amid stage effects of cannon bombardments and machine gun blasts, Romeo and Juliet are reborn in a world of identical Romeos and Juliets as though to say, 'Make Love, Not War,' and that love will never be dated."

---

112 Personal interview: Suzanne Farrell, 1974.

Suzanne Farrell again reminisced of the partnership she had had with dancer Jorge Donn, with whom she had danced the many ballets staged for her by Béjart: "Being here would have been sad were it not for Donn," she said. "You can't dance solos all your life, and its difficult to dance with someone you don't get along with. I trust Donn with my life. I know that if anything goes wrong, that he will help me. When he looks at you onstage, he *really* looks."

A second popular ballet for Farrell had been *Niiinsky, Clown de Dieu*. She remembered the numerous changes of costumes. "In *Niiinsky*, I danced the role of the Young Girl in Pink," she mused. "I was Béjart's feminine ideal that represented beauty, love, and security. But the ballet is about the stripping away of these things, as made visible by my costume. When *Niiinsky* begins, I wear this really gorgeous costume with a matching umbrella and pair of shoes. Each time I enter the stage my costume gets shorter; in the second act, I dance with the characters of each of the four clowns of Nijinsky, and then with Nijinsky himself."

In Europe, the ballet *Nijinsky, Clown de Dieu* had achieved a different audience reaction with each performance. In New York it wasn't presented as well. In Farrell's opinion, the performance of *Nijinsky* necessitated a stage that was circular in order to accentuate the choreography, conceived in circles. In Paris and in Brussels, a stage was designed so that four huge ramps led downward from its height into the audience. In New York, that 'feeling' wasn't there. A huge cross was placed in the arena of Madison Square Garden. Because the stage had no height, the scenic effect for the dancer was that of a cross that had been squashed.

Farrell concluded our interview by saying that she believed a choreographer really must know each dancer and that "certainly, the things that Béjart has choreographed for me have been special. Ballet is a hard life," she continued. "You give up many things." When Suzanne Farrell finally did leave Béjart, her dressing room was given to Angèle Albrecht. To many, it seemed as though an era of company history had passed.

DANIEL LOMMEL

Early in his career as a dancer, Daniel Lommel had refused to be molded by Béjart. With willpower and self-understanding, he taught himself first to dance and secondly, to dance with Béjart. One of the company's more versatile stars, he possessed a wry objectivity and, at all times, appeared at peace. Not originally trained as a dancer, Lommel had studied acting and design instead. Dance came later. "And," he said, "I began to see in dance all of the *plastique* which existed on the stage and in art."

In Paris, Lommel had studied with Nora Kiss. "In the beginning," he smiled, "I learned at least forty percent of what not to do in class. I was lazy; I liked to work, but not too much. I was also extremely weak. Nevertheless, I struggled to always do better than before, to always achieve a higher ideal. Today, I am thankful that my ambition was stronger than my attitude."

Lommel had seen Béjart's *Ballet Théâtre de Paris* in Liège, Belgium, and had performed with the company one month in Brussels for the premier in 1959 of *Le Sacré du printemps*. But after studying four years with Madame Nora, he chose to join the *Grand Ballet du Marquis de Cuévas*. Subsequently, with Janine Charrat, he toured America, but still did not perform with Béjart.

He came to Brussels when he felt ready in terms of his own experience as an artist. "I didn't want to go," he confided. "Before I do something, I have to know 'why.' Finally I felt ready to learn and to work with Maurice; to do what he wishes, but also to understand why. Now I am part of Maurice's idea. I have my own muscles, and my own head, but the grand design is his. I don't yet know," he confided, "if my presence here will produce a 'grand encounter.' I'm too close to the process to be objective and realize the role it will play in my life. Beyond the physical knowledge of sports, dance is an intense search into one's physical identity. To dance with Béjart is now to experience total joy physically, spiritually, and that akin to completing a personal *recherche*."

"Which role challenged you most?" I asked during our interview at the canteen in Béjart's studio in Brussels. "At a given moment," he answered, "each role will feel different. In some ballets, I was unhappy; not because of unchallenging roles, but because of not understanding their themes. Therefore, I learned to dance these ballets like writing a sentence, word by word. It wasn't always easy," he sighed. "Steps...one learns in class, but roles must be felt internally. What I most love to dance are roles that Maurice, himself, has created and danced."

As Lommel explained in our interview, "In *La Symphonie pour un homme seul,* the challenge is to interpret different layers of intensity used by the man to react against his environment. First he is violent, then he is calm, and finally he is wicked. It challenged me to imagine for myself a series of actions that would mimic words that are animal sounds and that for me, evoke situations that resemble the character. There is but one man and one woman in this ballet who react in tandem with men who perform as the crowd."

Lommel concluded by saying that Béjart was influenced by many things: by his culture, by his beginnings in Marseille, by his life, and all of its obstacles. It would be necessary," he stated, "to know him as he knows himself, to feel as he feels (and why), and to witness his evolution. Moreover," he added, "an exhuberance pervading the quality of knowledge he seeks is always present making it difficult to 'follow' him in the truest sense of the word. Of course," he concluded, "he has been positively influenced by travels and by poverty he has witnessed in India and in Mexico."

Lommel's favorite role was that of the Golden Slave in *Nijinsky, Clown de Dieu.* He described this role as symbolic of fire. "The slave," he mused, "truly has the qualities of flame, a being who never ceases to move and, thus, radiates." Like Suzanne Farrell, Lommel had danced in ballets choreographed both by Balanchine and by Béjart. "The only 'reproach' I can make of Balanchine," he added, "is that his choreography says little about himself or his soloists. He has created extraordinary ballets; yet the public is too often unaware and therefore unappreciative of their difficulty. Afterwards, it is wonderful to work with Maurice because he is close to character and to possibilities inherent in individuals. He makes his public aware of all which takes place, whether political, philosophical, or artistic.

"With people, Balanchine was fantastic; conversely Maurice, a human personality of our century, is at times inhuman with his dancers. He almost seeks to be unjust, knowing, perhaps, his action will produce a desired fantastic effect onstage. This is not intentional, but true. After Béjart, there is no one I truly know; if I were ever to leave his company, I would stop dancing."

"There are those who are close to him and those who feel more apart. With me, the closeness is more 'material' and of the moment; I want to learn roles, but when I am older, he will use me less and, as a result, we won't be so close. At times, there have been barriers between us, such as when he has told me I have danced poorly in a ballet when I feel I have danced well. That distresses me not because of my dancing, but because, in being close to him, I did not succeed. Yet, paradoxically, in this company, some are close to him all of the time. For these few, *Le Ballet du XXième Siècle* truly becomes a way of life."

JORGE DONN

When the company rehearsed for the evening-length spectacle work, *I Trionfi di Petrarca,* Jorge Donn clowned before the mirror, pretending to be a vamp. He pointed to a tear in his jeans, seductively ripping it open and calling out, "Ooh-la-la," as company members laughed . Relaxing following rehearsal at the canteen at Mudra, Donn and I were shielded from October's cold by heavy plastic strips which loosely dangled over the doorway. Donn autographed copies of *L'Autre Chant de la danse*, dedicated to him by Béjart. According to Donn, feelings revealed in the book were universal. Not only did they describe Béjart's perceptions, but also those of humanity. The symbols of the child in the forest, of the snowball that changes to crystal attached to the neck of a swan, the cool rainshower that gathers and washes all into oneness, are images which evoke personal interpretations.

When our interview took place, Mudrists were reading the chapter entitled, *Vénise*. After reading, they were to devise short skits using three or four dancers who would compete for a chance to perform in Venice at the First International Festival of Dance. Donn had been part of the company since the period of its inception. He had joined the company in 1964. Since then, he had interpreted many roles, portraying confused tormented heroes such as Petrarch, Romeo, and Faust. The role of Faust had become his *forte*. With dramatic presence, he had also performed with Jean Marais in a work entitled *L'Ange Huertebise* by Jean Cocteau. This performance by Donn had prompted a critic to comment:

> Who has not seen Marais writhe on the earth, evoking an angel's presence; who has not seen Jorge Donn in a long robe of muslin answer this call...cannot imagine how a movement can prolong the quality of feeling present in the poem. [113]

Born in Buenos Aires, Jorge Donn had made a pilgrimage from Argentina to dance with Béjart. He had danced as long as he could remember, enrolling first at the age of seven at the famed Teatro Colon and later appearing as Puck in *Le Songe d'une nuit d'hiver*. Until age sixteen, he had studied academic subjects in addition to performance, supporting his family for a time on the meager salary that he earned at the theater. He saw Béjart when the company visited Argentina to perform *Bolero* and *Le Sacré du printemps*. He knew that he had to join.

---

113 Andrè-Philippe Hersin, "A Bruxelles: Jean Cocteau et la danse" in *Les Saisons de la danse* (June, 1972), 8.

"Le Sacré du printemps amazed me," he said. "With Béjart, dance had become much more than simply raising a leg to a certain height. It was more and came from inside. There I was, at sixteen, wanting to join. But Maurice told me there was no position available. So they left Argentina, and I was sad. Since I come from a family of modest means, I borrowed from friends enough for the boat passage I then arrived in Brussels without a *sou*, but luck was with me. Béjart was astounded. Since someone in the company was ill, he took me immediately, paying me enough for room and board. I started by dancing in the *corps de ballet*.

"But when you dance for Béjart," he smiles, "you perform. He knows how to draw out of you things you are not yet conscious of knowing."

Jorge Donn had appeared in the ballet *Bhakti* in the role of Krishna, dancing to Indian sitar music. Once before in *Cygne*, he had mentioned Bejart's use of oriental harmonies to complement elaborate makeup that emphasized the dancers' eyes. Designed by Germinal Casado, the ballet had been one of the first to emphasize the presence of the male dancer.

In his own opinion, he had learned most from performing the role of Nijinsky. "The wonderful thing about Bejart," he said, "is that one participates in the choreographic act. Something created is something we do together; he doesn't prevent our own ideas from being heard. *Nijinsky, Clown de Dieu* was one of the important ballets I have danced. I believe a dancer must find his master and follow him; this is his most important mission. Each day I am grateful to have worked with such a person."

Donn's words separated him from contemporaries who had first danced with other companies. Whereas others preferred to train elsewhere and used Béjart's Brussels company as a final stepping-stone, Donn had devoted himself to one chosen master and had profited. "Before meeting Béjart," he paused, "I was nothing. He formed me, I did not exist before."

On November 30, 1991, at age forty-two, Jorge Donn died. His career resonated as an example of the modernist hero-as-dancer, envisioned by Béjart. Through seminal stage interpretations, such as *La Svmphonie pour un homme seul, Dichterliebe,* and *Faust,* Donn was the consummate Béjart dancer, embodying onstage a singular presence embued with an attitude of awakening and of revolt. As symbol of modernist hero, Donn evokes at once the dancer and the dance as conceived by Béjart. His performance can be defined as a duality created through reciprocal onstage surgings of alternative currents and forms.

CHAPTER FIVE
L'AUTRE CHANT DE LA DANSE

Some attempt must be made to account for recurring themes in Béjart's written work as they reappear with symbolic significance in his various ballets.His autobiography *L'Autre Chant de la danse*, published in 1974, recounts Béjart's childhood as perceived through recurring dream symbols of a continuous quest.

> ...it is very autobiographical. The main point is dreams; they are real dreams, and the second point...is a story of my youth, my first dance teacher, my father, my mother. Therefore, it is natural, since dreams are an expression of mine. 114

The problem of reference constantly faces the critic who must assess Béjart's theatricality. Understanding the intricate creative relationship between choreographer and dancer, his selection of literary themes, and their personal symbolic importance makes for exacting analysis. As a showman who manages to attract and elicit meaning from an array of opposing symbols, Béjart's eclecticism is multi-layered.

Béjart's images are devised to bring to the stage a part of his singular vision of the social-political relevance of the present through the exciting union of bodies, voices, and scenic effects. As a "literary" choreographer, Béjart's style might even be described as putting into practice archetypal reflections of works that *he* prefers. Béjart uses devices such as masks in *Notre Faust* to create irony, allowing him to deconstruct narrative form to enhance its status as archetype. He thus accentuated the use of a loudspeaker in *Serafita/Serafitus* and in *Notre Faust* to place himself as *auteur-director* within the narrative frame. In placing the self, subjectively, within the scenario, Béjart creates highly personal spectacles that abound with recurrent albeit intuitively legible archetypes. Originating within the realm of his subconscious, the destruction of

---

114 Personal Interview: Maurice Béjart, 1975.

the literary archetype, expressed as one reassembled as dance-spectacle, nevertheless remains enigmatic. Yet these recurrent archetypes reveal a seemingly continual force of energy and give his work vitality.

In *L'Autre Chant de la danse*, Béjart's autobiography, there is a sense of an unconscious fusing of dream symbols that recur as archetypes in his spectacle ballets. Furthermore, in reading this autobiography of dreams, we experience subjective elements of a coherent art entity. Béjart's personal phantasmagoria of imagery, expressed in his writing, is employed as a lingering dimension of his choreography. This subjective dimension tends to elicit deep antipathy from the spectator, particularly in ballets, such as *Notre Faust* or *Serafita/Serafitus* that distort the literary. Béjart's distortion of narrative form and image from works of literature to the "anti-performative" ballet spectacle can evoke feelings of hostility. Nevertheless, these distortions lend a certain banality and crude innocence to Béjart's work, displaying strengths and weaknesses at the same instant.

The text consists of 210 pages. Written during the early seventies, Béjart's autobiography describes a sequence of twelve dreams or symbolic recollections that relate to his childhood. It is also the first of three autobiographical texts written by Béjart, the one in which childhood appears most straightforwardly and in which it is most thoroughly explored.

In his collection of essays, *Man and His Symbols*, psychoanalyst Carl Jung describes dreams as revealing archetypes that evoke emotional responses, citing their recognition as cross-cultural. Just as the conscious mind imagines the future, the unconscious mind "acts out" or "practices" the future so that it may prepare for it through dreams. In one essay, Jung states that the ability to enunciate such a rich vein of material and effectively translate it into philosophy, literature, music, or even scientific discovery is one of the hallmarks of genius,[115] in rendering lucid the information contained in dreams. In his essay, "Maurice Béjart: The Sensual Moment," critic George Jackson remarked in the early eighties, that, "Up until 1972, from the visual evidence given, Béjart became involved with themes of dissolving the personality before gaining command of effective ways to achieve this on stage in dance." [116]

Until this period, Jackson continues, themes of love, war, aging, and learning have to do with losing the self. The hero, but one of Jung's archetypal figures, stands as an example of comparison with the lone figure, flanked by disjointed bodies, words, and gutteral sound. In *La Symphonie pour un homme seul*, the man stands alone, as he does in the ballets *Orphée and I Trionfi di Petrarca*. In these works not only must the hero be alone, but must also submit to a feminine twin or double. The feminine archetype of modernity present in Béjart's ballets represents that of the sister soul in movement evoking by necessity "the other," or "opposite" of the self, a feminine essence in constant transformation.

As icon of modernity Béjart's feminine archetype is varied. In *La Symphonie pour un homme seul* and in the third *pas de deux* of *Bhakti*, which is the portrayal of the romance of the Hindu god and goddess, Shiva and Shakti, the female dancer has a double identity: of companion and predator. In *Bolero*, as in the third *pas de deux* of *Golestan*, and in *Niiinsky, Clown de Dieu*, she appears as the goddess figure or representation of the shadow archetype understood by all, that emerges as part of a larger tapestry of the collective unconscious.

There are also archetypal themes. The theme of Love versus War is alluded to in Béjart's first ballet to the Faust legend, *Faust*, produced in Paris in 1966, and in *La Messe pour le temps présent*, produced in Brussels and Paris during the same period. In the early eighties, Béjart vividly criticized war in the spectacle work, *Wien*

---

115 Carl Jung, ed. *Man and His Symbols*. Essays quoted are by Joseph Henderson, "The Symbol as Modern Art," and by Aniela Jaffe, "Symbolism in the Visual Arts." Hereinafter abbreviated as MS.

116 Jackson, "The Sensual Moment," 1972.

Wien, Nur Du Allein, evoking images of Vienna. In this work, dancers, portraying emprisoned victims of war, groped against a backdrop suggesting bare brick walls covered with scribbled graffiti. Conversely, life and the erotic are explored as themes in such spectacle works as *Serait-ce la mort* and *Ce que l'Amour me dit*, danced to the music of Gustav Mahler's Third Symphony, echoing the late-century shift from modernism to post-modernism

If the archetype of self-dissolution informs ballets during the fifteen years following 1972, it does so most vividly in the final scene of the ballet *Romeo et Juliette*. There, dancers kneel on stage in pale white leotards and proclaim verbally to the audience, "Make Love, not War." What gives to *Romeo et Juliette* and other works of the period their thematic focus is the constant interplay of narrative that is implicitly portrayed and explicitly polarized as popular culture. Because narrative is present on two levels, it threatens to remain unresolved. Thus is the nature of dream. Though the intent of Béjart's ballet, like dreams, is often polyvalent and enigmatic, they nevertheless give the impression of a certain logic.[117] The irreality of dreams themselves, and Béjart's incessant desire as critic-voyeur to decipher their meaning through his creative dance spectacle, appears in *L'Autre Chant de la danse* in the second section of the book. Therein, dreamed passages represent the attempts of autobiography to reconcile the logical with the archetypal. Evident in *Serafita/Serafitus*, *Golestan*, and finally in the evening-length *Notre Faust*, the theme of the divided self is portrayed as the conscious self transcended through the dreamed or archetypal image.

In her essay, "The Symbol in the Visual Arts," Aniela Jaffe cites the conflict between the physical world and the spiritual world that first appeared as an influence on modernity in the years preceding World War I:

---

117 Béjart, *L'Autre Chant de la danse*, (Paris: Flammarion, 1974) 217-8. Hereinafter abbreviated as LC.

> From the psychological standpoint, the two gestures toward the naked object (matter) and the naked non-object (spirit) point to a collective psychic rift that created its symbolic expression in the years before the catastrophe of the First World War. This rift had first appeared in the Renaissance when it became manifest as a conflict between knowledge and faith. Meanwhile civilization was removing man further and further from his instinctual foundation, so that a gulf opened between nature and mind, between consciousness and unconsciousness. These opposites characterize the psychic situation that is seeking expression in modern art.[118]

As text, *L'Autre Chant de la danse* can be understood as Béjart's attempt to reconcile these opposites as literary representation, even as he transforms them as dance. The dreams in the first six chapters of the book are related as autobiographical anecdotes. Those in the succeeding four chapters, by contrast, which are described as "real." One might deduce that Béjart is indeed trying to form a logic founded on personal subconscious experience.

    L'Autre Chant de la danse deals with dreams as a rite of initiation. Although the typical hero figure must first exhaust himself in the process of achieving his goal, the hero of his narrative must give up all ambition and desire in the process of initiation. He must be willing to submit to the ordeal and, in essence, experience a trial without hope of success. Only by meeting obstacles and suffering pain, by enduring what Joseph Henderson, a Jungian, refers to as the "death experience," can one experience rebirth.[119] Thus, the poet-dreamer of *L'Autre Chant de la danse* achieves selfhood only in overcoming countless perils. The forest depths in *L'Ours*, the descending flight after encountering the god, Nijinsky, with a lamp in *Isisolde*, and the theater that bursts into flames in *La Callas*, all represent to the dreamer obstacles that he must transcend as he continues his quest, represented on the alchemical plane as change

---

118 MS, Jaffé "Symbolism in the Visual Arts," (New York: Doubleday, 1964), 253.
119 MS, Henderson "Ancient Myths and Modern Man," (New York: Doubleday, 1964), 131.

and transfiguration through fire. The sacred marriage, to which the dreamer is invited and that he is commanded to attend, symbolizes his attempt to reconcile his duality. The ballet enacts man's symbolic struggle to attain wholeness and communion between his physical and spiritual selves. Béjart's ballet images may represent a system of belief and of dream's instructive wisdom. What is most difficult to grasp, however, is Béjart's attempt to garner from the symbols of his dreamed experience, the totality of an aesthetic. For Béjart, each dance possesses derivative elements, yet each because of its expressive emotional symbolism is distinctly Béjart's own.

Béjart's dreams, expressed in *L'Autre Chant de la danse,* potentially may be classified into three categories, beginning with the personal image of the hero. It is the hero-as-poet who undertakes the Quest and who is accompanied at alternative intervals by each of three feminine alter-egos. These are symbolically represented in chapters entitled *Isisolde, Mae West,* and *La Callas.* Secondly, there are the places of encounter where the dreamer will encounter obstacles or receive some revelation. Each are analyzed, in turn. The places are the forest (in the chapter entitled *L'Ours*), the mosque in the middle of the desert (in *La Mosquée),* and the circus, represented by the dizzying encounter with Harpo Marx (in *Le Cirque*). As Mosques were often built with columns and vaults to emulate the medieval forest, both can be said to represent symbolically transformation or change. Thus, *L'Autre Chant de la danse* presents a series of complex images to the reader, in the quest for a sacred marriage of spirit and form, that represent the struggle in the psyche of Béjart. The power of the chapters resides in the mystical resolution of these dreams.

THE QUEST

As expressed in his writing, Béjart's philosophy is based on his fundamental belief in the self's ability to be redeemed. To arrive at a pure state of redemption, as symbolized by the sacred marriage of the unconscious and of the conscious self, or of soul and body, the dreamer must choose to embark on a quest, for spiritual wholeness and acceptance by the Supreme Self, who will emerge as the hero at the end of the cycle of transformation.

In the first chapter, entitled *L'Ours*, the dream begins with a dreamer recently awakened from deep sleep. "I awake and perceive near my side, a woman," he writes. The dreamer meets a female figure with green wings and three eyes, one of which rests, like that of the Cyclops, in the middle of her forehead. This female figure holds in her hand a leash to which is attached a lamb and a rose that she leaves with the dreamer. When she disappears, the dreamer encounters a second image: a swan.

The lamb, the dreamer realizes, is wounded. The blood gushing from his wound takes on the form of the rose that was left behind. This rose, in turn, metamorphosizes into a letter. The letter, presented both by the swan and the lamb, guides the dreamer. It indicates to him that a marriage will take place in a chateau toward which the dreamer must immediately depart.

The dreamer's solitude is is then broken by the arrival of François, who delivers a letter in which the correspondent refers to the present in the dreamer's psyche, underscoring the desire to dream and, through its guidance, to undertake a quest.

> L'obscurité est intense. Je ne vois plus rien; Je m'assieds sur le sol. Une surface polie s'illumine tout à coup. Je reconnais...mais oui, je suis au cinéma. [120]

> Obscurity is intense. I no longer see anything. Seated on the floor, a polished surface is illuminated suddenly. I understand... but yes, I am at the movies.

In the dreamer's cinema, he sees flames in which appear the vision of a child-self, a second important image. This child-self is a little boy

---

[120] Béjart, LC, 21.

who leads the dreamer from a forest, down a long road, to a wedding ceremony. In the forest, the dreamer senses that he is among people while, at the same time, he feels alone in their midst. Thus, he chooses not to ask questions, but to advance slowly. At one point, he must choose between two roads that he perceives as lines of a melody. "Do not take the path that the men in white direct you to take," he is told. "Take instead a pathway full of stones which proceeds in obscurity; do not be preoccupied by your solitude, but search!"[121]

As the two companions approach a windmill, their way is obstructed, and they are swept into its path. The child suggests that, to advance on the path toward the wedding ceremony, they become liquid. In the next series of images the dreamer envisions a King and the Queen seated together in the royal loge of the Opera.

Suddenly the King and Queen disappear, as does the theater or cinema. Although the theater is lost, the music remains. In this radically altered setting, the dreamer imagines his own birth.

> LE PREMIER JANVIER 1927
> La lumière.
> Un doigt d'or posé sur la fenêtre.
> Le Soleil.
> Le soleil est mon père.
> Malgré la nuit qui est en moi, je suis fils du soleil. Je dois le retrouver avant de parvenir au lieu des Noces, avant de rencontrer le Roi et la Reine, je dois parler avec mon père. [122]

> JANUARY 1, 1927.
> The Light.
> A golden finger leans on the window.
> The Sun.
> The Sun is my father.

---

121 Béjart, LC, 119.
122 Béjart, *LC*, 29.

> Despite the night that is in me, I am the son of the sun. I must
> find him before arriving at the place of the wedding ceremony,
> before meeting the King and the Queen, I must speak to my
> father.

Successive images of the mythical father within the dream setting
indicate the profound effect of this image on the dreamer. Moreover,
it is the father who leads the dreamer to regard dance as a sacred
initiation or rite. The dreamer and his father enter the forest together
and, asleep on its foliage, regard constellations in the sky that are
named after animals. The dreamer stares at the Big Dipper, otherwise
called *l'Ours* (the bear) when suddenly, from a forest thicket, a real
bear appears. Instead of being frightened, the dreamer befriends the
bear as a companion who will accompany him in the forest. This
companionship is sealed by a pact of movement enabling the dreamer
and his companion to travel together through the forest. The bear
enables the dreamer to better observe constellations in the sky. He
jumps on the animal's back, and they proceed through the forest
together. The bear then reveals a secret to the dreamer: he is the
oldest of twelve in a family including, among others: a tortoise, a
snail, a swan, and, of course, a snake.

    Then, alone in his room, the dreamer awakes. Psychoanalyst
Joseph Henderson writes that a child:

> possesses a sense of completeness, but only before the initial
> emergence of his ego-consciousness. In the case of the adult, a
> sense of completeness is achieved through a union of the
> consciousness with the unconscious contents of the mind. [123]

According to Jungians, the animal motif symbolizes man's primitive
and instinctual nature. Thus, before the dreamer completes the
symbolic union of the divided self, he must explore and uncover all
relics of his past. The journey through the forest represents this quest
just as the image of the the dance in the dream takes the dreamer by

---

[123] Jung, MS, 59.

surprise since it is conceived, at first, as having a purely animalistic function.

In the first dream, a singular characteristic is portrayed in Béjart's choreography of symbolical images that cross paths, but that often fail to connect. The swan, a symbol of transcendance, can be interpreted as man's intuition at work or, in the Wagnerian sense, as a harbinger of a sacred quest. The merging of the swan symbol with that of the bleeding lamb, however, suggests a plethora of spiritual images that must be understood interchangeably. At times, this degree of flux and imprecision obscures the quest, which forms the book's meaning.

Diffusion on one level is linked, in the reader's mind, with synthesis and analysis on another. One can get lost in the maze suggested by Béjart's symbols, or choose to regard the text as a whole conceived along the single design and symbolism of a quest during which the dreamer returns to childhood, acknowledges the self, then seeks a series of possible marriages or unions. Béjart's hero must meet with not one but three feminine alter-egos, presented in the forms of archetypes: *Isisolde, Mae West*, and *La Callas*.

THE POET MEETS MAE WEST

One of the more complex characteristics of Béjart's dance is his representation of women. His representation of the feminine archetype proceeds from the role of the vamp in *Symphonie pour un homme seul*, through that of the Girl in Pink in *Njiinsky, Clown de Dieu*, through numerous theater essays, such as *La Reine verte*. His modernist concept of woman represents her, respectively, as predator, mother, goddess, sister, and vamp. In some spectacle works, such as *Notre Faust*, she appears in several guises. *In L'Autre Chant de la danse*, she assumes no less than three forms and a chapter is devoted to each. Conversely, the image of her male companion might more simply be categorized as the poet whose duty it will be to serve as her receptacle. It is a Wagnerian axiom to describe the poet as the feminine receptacle impregnated by the masculine music. Béjart's stance resembles that of Wagner in that characterizations of the feminine expressed in chapters entitled *Isisolde, Mae West,* and *La Callas* do not woo the dreamer, but serve as emblems of the feminine, enabling him to undertake his quest.

As envisioned by Béjart, the dream autobiography thus assumes the countenance of continuous voyages that comprise a single, longer journey. Female figures purposefully guide the dreamer toward his own marriage that, for him, is deigned as sacred. In *Isisolde,* the companion to the dreamer appears as a winged woman with three eyes who presents to him a mysterious letter that summons him to a ceremony:

> Ce jour est celui des Noces Royales. Ta naissance t'y convie,
> tu es prédestiné à la joie...Isis. [124]

> This day is that of the Royal Marriage. Your birth requires
> your presence; you are predestined to joy....Isis.

The succession of images that prepare the dreamer to once again leave his room to embark on a mystical journey introduce Isis, the veiled goddess, and Isolde, sister-companion to Tristan as one feminine archetype. The dreamer's room, represented as the station terminus of the Orient Express, is dominated by the presence of *Isis* who beckons the dreamer to begin the journey. The image then changes abruptly from a sailboat that passes a bridge each evening shortly after midnight to a chateau that disappears and reappears every forty years. Yet the most curious image is one that alludes to Nijinsky, the dancer. Undoubtedly due to Béjart's contemporaneous choreography of *Nijinsky, Clown de Dieu,* Nijinsky is one of the few figures described seriously. He appears as a man dressed in white holding a lamp, symbolizing the figure of the hermit and guide. To the dreamer, Nijinsky is climbing what he describes as "invisible gradations of stairs" that lead upward into a temple. The dreamer himself chooses to explore its depths, crossing a hallway on his knees toward the entrance.

This chapter takes on an aspect of fantasy as it centers on the dreamer's discovery of a diary written by the famed *Ballets Russes* dancer Nijinsky. In the diary are written two underlined words: *La Mort* and *La Folie*. The discovery is a significant turning point because the dreamer must choose. He is confronted once again with duality. As he arrives at the gate of the temple, he is pulled upward by a cord and freed in the open space of a vestibule where twelve lamps burn. There, twenty-two frescoes, each endowed with a letter, align themselves in an immense empty gallery. The frescoes form an enigma, yet it is one familiar to the dream.[125]

Sensing that time is limitless, the dreamer attempts to decipher the meaning of the frescoes and plucks from one of them a marguerite. As he does so, he hears the voice of a child singing nonsensical rhymes of five couplets recounting a tale of fallen leaves. One verse that begins, *Mais une feuille énervée* (But a rustling leaf) is succeeded by another that continues, *Mais une feuille encore vierge* (But a leaf that is still green). The rhyme concludes with a final verse that begins, *Mais une feuille grande comme la Chine et couverte d'encre verte n'a pas d'odeur malgré les cornes de Vénus et les soupirs de la Pléiade* (But a leaf as large as China, covered with green ink that has no odor in spite of the hornes of Venus and sighs of the Pléiade).[126]

In the following scene, the dreamer imagines himself amid red flames of Stravinsky's *L'Oiseau de feu* in the supposed security of an opera house stage. Although the voice ceases to sing, orange tissues animated by artificial winds, representing a sudden burst of flame depict the dreamer's fantasy. In a frenzy, the dreamer is summoned to dance and rushes from the theater. He returns to the night before by plunging into an invisible lake where he perceives a

---

125 Béjart, *LC,* 50.
126 Ibid.

woman standing on a barge who is surrounded by eleven lamps. Aware that she will rescue him, he climbs onto the vessel to sail away with her toward an alternative, but unknown destination.

In the chapter entitled *Isisolde*, one may sense an attitude or mood of transcendence from the physical to the spiritual world that is also present in the final act of ballets such as *Serait-ce la Mort* or *Romeo et Juliette*. Beckoned by the chant of an unnamed woman, who sails on a barge, the dreamer is enveloped by a sense of mystic communion symbolized by the presence of water. Like the windmill of the first dream, it allows him, by its liquid form, to follow its path. The presence of the woman on the barge assures that the dreamer's quest is transparent and will continue beyond the theater's stage toward his ultimate goal of the sacred marriage ceremony that represents wholeness and true awareness of self.

Mae West becomes the second most significant female image encountered by Béjart's voyager. In the third dream, the opening image is of the dreamer in his room where he will receive a new invitation to which he must immediately respond. Once again, the dreamer is told he is wanted "without delay," at the chateau where the King and the Queen will celebrate their marriage. Only this time, the guide is not a swan, but a pelican who carries the letter in his beak. The pelican tells the dreamer that only "perhaps" will he obtain the key to the door that will open the chateau. On a barge arranged with cushions and emitting strange perfumes, Mae West appears. For a brief moment the dreamer is deceived. *Certainement son corps est le château. La cérémonie des noces est facile* (Certainly her body is the castle; the nuptial ceremony is easy), he exclaims.[127]

With outstretched arms and "a small pudgy hand whose fingernails are painted brilliant red," Mae West summons the dreamer. But the latter is held back by the pelican who digs his beak into the dreamer's ankle. Making a sign to Mae West, the pelican

---

127 Béjart, *LC,* 60.

grasps the leaves of a tree as Mae West departs toward the sea on the barge.

At this point, the dream functions as a sacred ritual. It is as though the presence of Mae West, a goddess figure, necessitates affirmations of piety. In succeeding images, the dreamer sees a procession of young boys and girls who hold in one hand a candle and in the other a peacock feather. Among those participants in the procession is a little boy of four or five years. Entirely nude, he wears a serpent around each wrist. He exchanges with the dreamer one serpent for a rose. Immediately, the other nibbles at the dreamer's ear and tells him one day he will see a name inscribed on water and that, after drinking this water, he must search for the sap of a wild olive tree. Only in drinking this liquid will he cease to walk on the desert and will he hear wild animals call the praises of the sun. Only after drinking this sap will the dreamer truly know his father. Until then, the serpent continues, the dreamer must kneel at each crossroad and collect three stones and seven flowers. He must then wait for the passing of nine birds. At each point, as the dreamer continues his journey. Whenever the dreamer seems tired, the serpent will nibble at each ear to remind him of his quest. Finally, at daybreak, the dreamer reaches a crossroad where he sees a statue of St. Bernard. As he prays in front of this statue, the brilliant light of seven angels confronts him. One of the angels stabs the dreamer with his sword. As he falls, he is conscious of the serpent still nibbling at his ear and remembering the spectre of the angels, muses: *Il faut risquer avant d'atteindre le point où l'on goûte la pure essence de l'amour* (One must risk before attaining the point where one tastes love's pure essence). The dreamer sighs and experiences a short-lived peace before a dragon appears who is about to devour the dreamer. He awakens, startled.[128] . When the dreamer opens his eyes, however, he is again in his room where the heat has been turned off. It is raining. The serpent whispers again:

---

128 Béjart, *LC, 65.*

Ne cherche pas à comprendre pour croire, mais crois afin de comprendre. Persuadé que si tu ne crois pas d'abord, tu ne comprendras jamais. [129]

Do not seek to understand to believe, but believe to understand. Be persuaded that if you do not first believe, you will never understand.

In this third dream, the dominating presence is the serpent. Both Mae West and the serpent function as symbols of seduction. The dreamer resists, but still chooses to continue his quest to witness the sacred ceremony. This dream, as Béjart reveals it to us, is also represented in the spectacle *Notre Faust*, and is indigenous to the Faust legend. It functions to assert that only through temptation and the experience of evil will one be guided toward redemption. On another plane, the inacessibility of Mae West and the terrifying presence of angels are of interest as they reveal the multiple fears that torment the dreamer.

In the chapter entitled *La Callas*, the dreamer's room is transported into the opera loge. As he sleeps, La Callas steals the letter from the dreamer, while at the foot of his bed a swan sings of the sad, unhappy love of a pelican for a golden rose. Here Béjart, as the dreamer, plays humorously. The subconscious essence of Maria Callas, the Italian diva, is expressed through symbolical presence of a swan, a rose, and a pelican. This essence communicates to him that his sister soul resides in Greece and causes the dreamer to mount the highest rafters of the theater and jump from its balcony into the courtyard of a mosque.

After the dreamer kneels on a rug in prayer, he discovers his rug has been transformed into a flying carpet that can carry him through water and air to a countryside of cliffs, edifices, and trees that resemble the countryside of Greece. Marching among a group of young men, the dreamer continues his quest in search of a mythical "Sophia," the name given his sister soul by La Callas. During this

129 Béjart, *LC*, 72.

dream the dreamer wakens, then returns to sleep, wondering if he has dreamed. When he is asleep the second time, he envisions the theater being destroyed by flames. Only La Callas is unharmed. She tells the dreamer,

> Tu parcours un curieux chemin. Tu fais des zigzags, un pas en avant, deux en arrière. Où vas-tu?
> "Je ne sais pas, je cherche."
> Sophia? Je ne crois pas que tu réussiras à la trouver. Pour cela il te faudrait le Feu, mais un feu différent de celui qui vient de brûler ce théâtre.
> "Ce théâtre est mort."
> Il y a en toi un autre théâtre. Trouve-le, extirpe-le et brûle-le. [130]

> You are following a curious road. You make zigzags, one step ahead and two backwards. Where are you going?
> "I do not know, I seek."
> Sophia? I do not believe you will find her. To do so, you will need Fire, but a different fire from that which destroyed this theater.
> "This theater is dead."
> In you dwells a different theater. Find, eradicate, and burn it.

In the constantly changing texture of the encounter with *La Callas* the dreamer first flies through the air on a carpet before swimming in water like an ondine-sprite. He is quite conscious of the meaning of his quest, revealed as four trials of alchemical elements of fire, water, earth, and air; yet conversely experiences a need for repose. Only when he encounters the ideal realm can he rest and consider his quest fulfilled. He has been guided toward the place of the sacred union by a trio of three of his sister-souls: *Isisolde, La Callas,* and *Mae West.*

---

130 Béjart, *LC,* 90.

161

THE PLACE OF THE CEREMONY

In Béjart's world, dualism stems from his dreams of childhood along with his personal quest for a sacred union of masculine and feminine selves. Before the tension produced by this dualism can be resolved, the dreamer of the fifth dream will be led to the desert where a mosque will be constructed.

To construct a mosque takes time, the dreamer is told. In this dream, the dreamer has no bedroom, but has chosen to live within the sacred ruins of a temple. Only after many years, when he sees a carp struggling to stay alive in the desert, will the dreamer choose to rebuild the mosque so that the carp may live. The work is arduous and long. He must obtain cement and gravel from a village far away and walk many miles each day. Nevertheless, the dreamer undertakes the task of rebuilding: *Enfin, après des années de travail, d'obstination, de folie, de sagesse, la Mosquée existe* (After many years of work, obstination, madness, and wisdom, the Mosque exists).[131]

> In this dream, one can sense the importance of the relationship of time. Only after years of work can the mosque be rebuilt and, once built to resemble something the dreamer has known before. In Béjart's case, this dream may relate to the past and to the childhood dream of becoming the dancer that he could never be.[132]

Finally, the dreamer decides he must build a bridge over an imaginary stream where he sees the carp swimming. Since Béjart's conversion to Islam has occured during the same chronological period as the writing of *L'Autre Chant de la danse*, the construction of a bridge is significant. Scholar Arthur Jeffery writes in *Reader on Islam*, "All people will be sent to the Bridge after they have been

---

131 Béjart, *LC*, 99.
132 Personal Interview: Violette Verdy, 1978.

standing around the Fire, and will cross the Bridge according to their works."[133]

Thus, in Béjart's final dream, the construction of a bridge represents the culmination of a personal vision and desire for fulfillment. Only after the construction of the bridge that the significance of the Road be made apparent and fulfillment achieved. After the dreamer crosses it to arrive at the first village, he sees a wedding ceremony take place. The dreamer may then return to his room at peace.

Béjart alludes to a dream within a dream. The invitation seems ridiculous: a dream to the dreamer: *Quelqu'un a voulu se moquer de moi* (Someone wanted to make fun of me), he calls. *J'ai pourtant le sentiment très net de devoir accomplir un voyage à la recherche de...*(Still, I feel I must carry out a voyage to the remembrance of ...).[134] The dreamer then enters a chateau, wherein he perceives a table around which are seated twelve persons, among them Gustave Moreau, Novalis, and Harpo Marx. The dreamer appears to know them as friends. Continuing on the road, the dreamer passes a cemetery and discovers a tomb inscribed with the name, Sophie:

> Sophie est là, morte. Non, Sophie est vivante, vivante pour toujours en moi. Cette mort présumée n'est que le prélude de la vraie vie. Je me baisse, embrasse la tombe et me sens soudain plein d'une joie intense. [135]

> Sophie is there, dead. No, Sophie is alive, alive forever in me. This presumed death is only the prelude for true life. I lower myself to embrace the tomb and suddenly feel myself full of intense joy.

---

133 Arthur Jeffery, *Reader on Islam* (S-Gravenhage: Mouton, 1962) 73.
134 Béjart, *LC*, 101.
135 Béjart, *LC*, 124.

Leaving the cemetery, the dreamer returns to the vision of night, and to the memory of his father. He approaches a final crossroads where the words: *La Mort appelle les noces* (Death calls forth the wedding ceremony) are inscribed. Proceeding, he enters a cavern where, upon opening a door, he sees a child who is learning to dance.

This little boy, who is called Leonardo, knows the dreamer. The dreamer, in turn, gives the boy a dance lesson and tells him that, above all else, he must seek a special relationship with a certain *Belle* who is really the personification of the *barre* of the ballet class. Equally, he must be aware of the mirror that is deceitful but, like a faithful dog. Also, he must not forget the floor. Hearing the music of a harp, Leonardo begins to dance. Harpo then leads the dreamer toward the symbolic ceremony. Once again in his room, the dreamer sleeps as Harpo plays the piano and Leonardo draws an imaginary rose. A comparison of the setting in *La Mosquée* with that of the following dream, *Venise*, reveals an abrupt difference in texture due to a shift from religious symbols to an expressive use of collage. Accompanied by both Harpo and Leonardo, his alter-egos, the dreamer travels to Venice. En route, he keeps a notebook where he records, piecemeal, a strange uncanny ritual from a previous dream.

> Lorsque la lune aura paru dans le ciel, tue le Roi, égorge la Reine, et appelle les valets afin que leurs corps soient rituellement embaumés. Ensuite, demande au chat qui garde le donjon, le chemin du bois sacré. 136

> When the moon appears, kill the king, cut the queen's throat, and call the servants so that their bodies may be ritualistically embalmed. Then, ask the cat who guards the dungeon the way to the sacred forest

In Venice, Harpo awaits on the *quai* of the Grand Canal with a rose. The two proceed to the *Casino des Esprits* as the dreamer fades quickly into a series of paintings, the last of which depicts a circle of

---

136 Béjart, *LC*, 119-20.

women embroidering a tapestry. Recognizing the face in the tapestry as his own, the dreamer seizes a needle and pricks his finger. Subsequently, he drowns in a single drop of blood only to awaken abruptly as though in prison. Through its bars, he sees a mosque near a bridge. Falling to his knees, he hears a woman's voice:

> Ce qu'il fallait faire, tu as oublié, c'était planter autour de la mosquée un jardin de roses. [137]

> What you should have done, you have forgotten; you should plant a rose garden around the mosque.

He recognizes the voice as that of the temptress Mae West. When the dreamer inquires about Harpo, Mae West tells him that she cannot appear in the same film as he, and quickly disappears.

Once again the dreamer finds himself *en route* to an unknown destination. He is on the train and is traveling to Venice when, spying a laurel bush, he jumps from the window of the wagon-lit to caress the flowers. He remarks, "It seems that I eat my own flesh. This liquid that fills my mouth is blood." From the sky, he hears a voice that says, "The twelfth is my beloved son in whom I have placed my hopes."[138] Taking the vase in his right hand he raises it three times above his head. Then, covering it cautiously with the other hand, he presses it hard against his chest and returns to the depths of the forest.

The *Interlude* which follows the first five dreams of *L'Autre Chant de la danse* is significant. The dreamer has identified his search and finds himself in a room crowded with objects, some from his present and some from his memory. While Harpo sleeps at the foot of the dreamer's bed, the dreamer recites a prayer from the Koran, sensing the health and wisdom of God. Suddenly the dreamer feels the need to depart from the past, even though he laments the loss

---

137 Béjart, *LC,* 123.
138 Béjart, *LC,* 130.

of some object or some person. Perhaps the sole goal of human life, he concludes, is to discover the divine.[139]

Although the first six dreams of *L'Autre Chant de la danse* expressly deal with self discovery, they also heavily focus on Béjart's need to explore and thus to know his past and, in so doing, know the world of his father. Situated before the *Interlude,* that begins as a stream of consciousness dialogue, the dreams are rich with texture and imagery. In contrast, the succeeding four dreams originate in actual memory: *Le Cirque* calls to mind images of the actress Mathé Souverbie who performed lead roles in *La Reine verte*; *Seraphiel* and *La Princesse*, in turn, focus upon the feminine image, or an androgynous self Béjart idolizes. Perhaps the most touching of these dreams is entitled *Elle*. This dream forms a composite image of a ballet school in Marseilles where, as a little boy, Béjart learned to dance. *Ma chambre est en moi* (My room is inside me),[140] the dreamer declares.

In Béjart's text, thought and fantasy in the final four dreams symbolize the father figure, while, conversely, instinct in the former dreams alludes to the mother. When, by the eleventh chapter, the dreamer's quest is defined, his journey ends. Having arrived at *L'Isle verte* (the Emerald Isle), the dreamer has fulfilled his quest. In this final chapter, all images of sense contained in preceding dreams: a garden, a walk, a country, a meal, a rose, music, dance, a vibration, are well defined, although the dreamer confesses that it is through the act of writing that he is able to achieve a very personal quest.

Béjart totally surrenders to experience and, in so doing, makes clear an intense, personal network of symbols that mark his dances. The world of *L'Autre Chant de la danse* originates in the imagination. Its characters, while dissociated, are given a special and completely personal meaning. Béjart's spectacle art desires that the spectator return to his own beginnings, with the dream surrounding birth since,

---

139 Béjart, *LC*, 136.
140 Béjart, *LC*, 181.

according to Jung, birth occurs before a sacred marriage between the ego and the self can take place.

Then, guiding the spectator through images of a sister-soul, respectively revealed as *Isisolde*, *La Callas*, and *Mae West*, he invites the spectator to share his personal vision and wisdom. In the second dream, Béjart discovers in the pages of *Nijinsky's Diary* two words: *La Folie* or "livingness" and *La Mort* or Death. Representation in Béjart's choreography is articulated in terms of these symbols and made lucid through spectator participation. As Béjart was to say during the course of our visit, "Dreams are an expression of mine."[141]

At the end of the quest, the dreamer must undergo one more trial. In the final scene of *La Mosquée*, the dreamer, the little boy Leonardo, and Harpo return to the dreamer's chamber only to arrive once again at a point of new becoming.

> Je pense à la mosquée dans le desert, mon voyage, quel est le but de tout cela? [142]

> I think of the mosque in the desert, my voyage, what is the end of it all?

In his room, seated on a corner of the bed, Leonardo draws a rose while, Harpo, standing against a library shelf, caresses an invisible harp:

> Je ferme les yeux.
> L'abandon.
> Lui sait.
> Dieu est le plus grand. [143]

141 Personal Interview; Maurice Béjart, 1977.
142 Béjart, *LC*, 113.
143 Ibid.

I close my eyes.
Abandon,
He knows.
God is the highest.

CONCLUSION

During latter decades of the twentieth century, when growing curiosity about dance has caused this art form to compete with theater, cinema, and opera for popularity, Béjart's *Ballet du XXième Siècle* emerged as a macrocosm of virtual theater. His spectacle ballets drew their impulses more from historical trends in *mise-en-scène* espoused by such multi-theatrical systems as the *Ballets Russes* of Diaghilev, the theatrical system espoused by Antonin Artaud, the post-war theater, and early modern dance spectacle, than from classical ballet. From the latter, Béjart has taken his technical base, while at the same time rebelling against its conventions and classicism through innovative experiments with sound, *mise-en-scène,* and movement, celebrated through subtly shifting fantasies of montage.

As an expression of mid-twentieth century modernism, Béjart's quest was to free the art of dance, and particularly the ballet, from a restricting system of codes, and dialectically to incorporate other distinct mediums into dance forms. In doing so, Béjart's dance creations become hybrids, establishing in their wake a form of multi or virtual theatrical event. Through staging practices of dance as a principal element, interpretation becomes possible as recognition of a series of distinct *auteuristic* signatures. The basic text of the literary work may serve, as in the case of ballets such as *Notre Faust, L'Oiseau de feu, Nijinsky, Clown de Dieu,* and *Baudelaire,* as archetype, one that is fused into a subtext of writerly symbols. Spectators, then, are compelled to engage in thoughtful reflection to decipher their meaning.

The art of Béjart may be said to propose an alternative tradition, neither categorized as, nor derivative of the art form whose name appears in either title as 'ballet.' Whether titled *Ballet du*

XXième Siècle or Béjart Ballet Lausanne, his art of the mid-twentieth century triumphed as an expressive vision of modernism in dance. As a confluence of forms, it receives its impetus from the deconstruction of the literary narrative, a mutation processed through continuous codes that culminated and explored in its wake historical and current events, thereby allowing positive 'destruction,' revolution, and change within parameters of the dance art form.

As a forerunner of an alternative tradition, the great audience Béjart once envisioned in America remained a chimeric quest.. In the company's early performances in the latter decades of the century, ballets such as *Bhakti* and *Messe pour le temps présent* proposed to deliver truth slogans often termed as *cliché.* (Examples are the final scene of *Romeo et Juliette,* that contained, in the manner of a sixties ritual chant, the plea 'Make Love, Not War;' or in *Bhakti,* where dancers parading onstage assumed the guise of Hare Krishna devotees).

Yet, in later decades, the metaphorical title, *Ballet du XXième Siècle* assumed deeper meaning as Béjart's continuously changing aesthetic became more than a channel for slogans. Performers of both companies changed the parameters of classical dance, displaying boundless commitment and versatility, representing through variance of tone, a cultural difference of dance reception.

By the eighties Béjart had created hybrid choreographies and engaged in new realms of corporal expression. Targeting the artist/dancer's ascent as hero, forging through danced performance the barest threads of the modernist parable of struggle in modern life, Béjart's seminal works, at once metaphorical and psychological, proffered a unique view of their present. As such, these stagings of the mid- to late-twentieth century burst forth as intense self-probing that used danced form as their central element to reveal the disparate contexts of the present.

In Béjart's works, dance is devised not only as an art form unto itself, but one that is co-dependent on several systems of meaning encompassing the literary, the psychological, and the semiotic. Béjart's staging is complex, at times working with *mise-en-abîme* or within frames that create, then destroy, before engaging in processes of performance (such as in the 1992 spectacle performance in Lausanne of Béjart's directing Patrice Chereau, who—as director—in turn encounters cultural heroes of mythic proportions: Mishima and Eva Peron). Thus, as spectators observing a spectacle that presents itself as multi-theater and as *mise-en-abîme,* we witness multiple layers of meaning.

Incessant and honest, Béjart's probing is at once actual and autobiographical. Whether or not one admits the validity of his quest, one admires his force and audacity and force. Certainly, the personal vision inherent in works such as *Notre Faust, Serafita/Serafitus,* and *Dichterliebe,* has destroyed what began as *authorly* text only to reveal a truer essence through processes of destruction.

In Béjart's entourage, one dancer concluded, performance becomes a way of life; yet, in being *prospective,* Béjart's dance embraces both the essential present of dance and its future. As staged works, ballets such as *Le Sacré du printemps, Pli selon pli,* and *L'Oiseau de feu* have survived to become part of a repertory reifying the hybrid form that, enduring a season or two, is rarely restaged in exactly the same way. As part of a progression of multi-theatrical systems, Béjart's work may influence choreographers and stage directors of the future who, like Béjart, will be inspired to transform past creations. From the diversity and energy of the spectrum on which it is based, Maurice Béjart's art of the mid-twentieth century progressed as a tribute to the constant, eclectic fusion of the moment, expressed as a singular expression of modernism in art.

BIBLIOGRAPHY

----------------. "Evolution of La Loie's Dance," in *The New York Herald.* (August 27, 1893). Reprint: San Francisco Archives For The Performing Arts, 1977.

Apollinaire, Guillaume. *L'Enchanteur pourrisant.* Paris: Gallimard, 1972.

--------------, *L'Esprit nouveau et les poètes.* Paris: Gallimard 1974.

Bablet, Denis. *Le Décor du théâtre contemporain.* Paris: Editions Centre National de la Recherche Scientifique, 1965.

Banes, Sally. *Writing Dancing In the Age of Post-Modernism.* New England: Wesleyan, 1994

Cawelti, J.G. "Notes Toward an Aesthetic of Popular Culture." *Journal of Popular Culture*: 3 (1972).

Christout, Marie-Françoise. *Béjart.* Paris: Chiron, 1988.

Cavell, Stanley. *The World Viewed.* New York: Viking, 1972.

Derrida, Jacques. *L'Ecriture et la différence.* Paris: Seuil, 1967.

Garaudy, Roger. *The Alternative Future.* Trans: Leonard Mayhew. New York: Simon & Schuster, 1974.

-------------------. *Danser Sa Vie.* Paris: Seuil, 1973.

Henderson, Joseph. *The First Avant-Garde (1887-1894).* London: George G. Harrap, Ltd., 1971.

Higgins, Kathleen. "Nietzsche on Music," in *Journal of the History of Ideas,* 47:4. Baltimore: Johns Hopkins University Press, 1986, 663.

Jasper, George. *Adventure in the Theater.* Rutgers: Rutgers University Press, 1947.

Jeffery, Arthur. *A Reader on Islam.* New York: S-Gravenhage: Mouton, 1962.

Jullian, P. *Dreamers of Decadence.* New York: Praeger, 1971.

Jung, Carl, ed. *Man and His Symbols.* New York:
   Doubleday Anchor, 1964.

Kirby, E.T., ed. *Total Theater.* E.P. Dutton, 1969.

Lehmann, A.G. *The Symbolist Aesthetic in France: 1885-1895.*
   London: Basil Blackwell, 1965.

Leonard, A.R. *A History of Russian Music.* New York
   MacMillan, 1957.

Levinson, André. *The Story of Léon Bakst's Life.* Berlin: Russian
   Art Publishing, 1922.

Livio, Antoine. *Béjart.* Paris: La Cité, 1970.

Merlin, I. *Poètes de la révolte de Baudelaire à Michaux.* Paris:
   L'Ecole, 1970.

Nataf, Raphael. "La Reine verte." In *Théâtre Populaire.* 52:3 (1963), 103
   -105.

Peyre, Henri ed. *Baudelaire: A Collection of Critical Essays.*
   New York: Prentice Hall, 1962.

Polanyi, Michel. *The Tacit Dimension.* New York: Doubleday,
   1968.

Propert, W.A. *The Russian Ballet in Western Europe: 1909-1920.*
   London: John Lane, 1921

Reiss, Françoise. *Nijinsky ou la Grâce.* Paris: Editions d'Histoire
   Et d'Art, 1957.

Révue Wagnerienne, VI (1885-1886), Geneva: Slatkin
   Reprints, 1968, 159-164.

Scandura, Jani and Thurston, Michael, eds. *Modernism, Inc.*
   New York: NYU Press, 2001.

Wilson, Edmond. *Axel's Castle.* New York: Scribners, 1945.

INDEX